Lessons from the Land
of Pork Scratchings

Lessons from the Land of Pork Scratchings

How a Miserable Yank Discovers the Secret of Happiness in Britain

GREG GUTFELD

POCKET
BOOKS

LONDON • SYDNEY • NEW YORK • TORONTO

First published in Great Britain by
Simon & Schuster UK Ltd, 2008
This edition first published by Pocket Books, 2009
An imprint of Simon & Schuster UK Ltd
A CBS COMPANY

1 3 5 7 9 10 8 6 4 2

Simon & Schuster UK Ltd
1st Floor
222 Gray's Inn Road
London WC1X 8HB

www.simonsays.co.uk

Simon & Schuster Australia
Sydney

A CIP catalogue record for this book
is available from the British Library

ISBN: 978-1-84739-075-2

Typeset by M Rules
Printed by CPI Cox & Wyman, Reading, Berkshire RG1 8EX

CONTENTS

For Elena

ACKNOWLEDGEMENTS

I would like to thank my lovely wife, Elena, who put up with all my nonsense while writing this book, and willingly accepted all the episodes of afternoon drinking required to do that. I also apologize to her for my pathetic weight gain and the body odour it has caused.

I would like to thank Eugenie Furniss for approaching me to do this book – even though every time we met we never talked about the book, only about some guy you were dating. That's OK – but you should have drunk more.

I would like to thank Kerin O'Connor, who approached me to come to *Maxim*. You had great faith in me, and I will always count you as a dear friend who wears too many scarves. Also, Bruce Sandell, for hiring me – and firing me! Also, Felix. I enjoyed all those precious moments you yelled at me. Special thanks to the great Phil Hilton, a marvellous person who openly ridiculed me at a dinner party over my mispronunciation of Evelyn Waugh's last name. I forgive you. Also, to Kevin Godlington, to Sam Delaney – so British, if you slice him open he bleeds crumpets. Also, Camilla Wright, for being a fun drinking buddy and taking me and Elena to Ascot. I still owe you £60. Also, David Whitehouse, the best writer weighing under five stone. Eoin McSorely, whose pleasant demeanour is matched only by his misguided politics. Neil Stevenson, for the karaoke and the handcuffs. James Brown, for advice I never listened to.

Special thanks to all the great and talented people at *Maxim* and Dennis, like Chris Bourn, Jenni Davis, Alex Godfrey, Nick Leftley, Steve Neaves, Martin Robinson, Darren Siveter, Joe Frost, Cat Costello, Jason Timson, Jimi Famurewa, Mike Dent, Richard Bean, and anyone else I might have forgotten!

Paul Mauro and Alison Rosen for advice and suggestions as

well as Jane Bussman, Andy and Carolyn Clerkson, Aric Webb, Ron Geraci, Denis Boyles, Mark Golin, Fox News, Scott Norvell.

Also, Kerri Sharp, my editor, who'd better make me look smarter than I actually am (not a tough feat). Also, the bartenders at the King and Queen and the King's Arms, the staff at the Groucho, who keep sending me bills, and my mom, for having me.

Some material in this book appeared in features I wrote for other publications. Portions of the chapter ASBOs, as well as stuff about weight gain first appeared in *FHM* in 2006, when the great editor and Phil Collins lookalike Ross Brown hired me as a monthly columnist. I would especially like to thank him for that; it helped get me through the summer without a real job. I would also like to thank him for pushing me around the *FHM* building in an office chair at midnight while screaming drunk. Portions from the chapter on two-pence coins came from my monthly column in the *American Spectator*, as well as a few sentences here and there, near the end, on Johnny Rotten. I would like to thank Amspec for supporting my work, as well as giving me my first job out of college. If it wasn't for them, I would probably be a success. The chapter on the bombings in London initially began as a letter to my friend Jessica Coen at Gawker, written on the day of the attack, and a description of a typical day at work originally appeared in Campaign, which I expanded upon in this book into something that is probably completely different but I can't remember because it's really late when I'm writing this and I've drunk too much.

In some chapters names have been changed because I didn't want to get anyone in trouble. And in some cases I didn't remember their names at all. Which brings me to chronology and things like the names of sandwiches: I tried my very best to depict my life in England as accurately as possible. I admit this was on occasion something of a challenge, because for the most part I was drinking. Yes, I am implementing alcohol as an excuse for any and all inaccuracies.

INTRODUCTION

When I was first approached to write a book about my experiences as a Yank in Britain, I was fairly certain I had nothing extraordinary to say. After all, there were no huge dramatic incidents that caused tremendous epiphanies. I never got arrested, mugged or beaten up. I did throw up once, but that was from food poisoning.

If anything, for me, the most remarkable thing about being in England was how much didn't happen. The only thing I could point out for sure that occurred was a significant transformation in my mental outlook. I became happier. And so that's what this book is about: how a Yank finds the secret to happiness in the land of blood pudding, scotch eggs and Jeremy Paxman.

But first there needs to be some clarification. It's true that I found happiness. But I kept finding it in the same place. Meaning, the pub. So do not be alarmed if seventy to eighty per cent of the action takes place in musty rooms with tacky carpeting and farting dogs. This should be no surprise to smart people and drunks. The pub allows for contemplation and conversation, the two most important elements in forming productive thoughts about life. It also helps to have Stella on tap, the Jam on the jukebox and a pack of Marlboro Lights in your pocket.

Oh yes, ciggies . . . that's another thing I need to sort out. One of the central keys to my happiness in London was smoking. Bliss for me was a pack of smokes and a pint at the King's Arms on Riding House Street, London at 3 p.m. Smoking in pubs plays a big part in this book, even though it no longer does in your life. Smoking is now banned in pubs, and for that I am truly sorry. But I read recently that now there is no smoking in British pubs, the stench of sweat, stale beer and flatulence, normally camouflaged by the billows of exhaled smoke, has revealed its ugly self to all the repulsed patrons. That's the price you pay for legislating away a good time.

And speaking of a good time, I hope you have one while reading this book. If you don't, I don't want to hear about it.

1. THE LIFE COACH

I see Joe's perfect sandy blond hair from where I'm standing – he's sitting in the restaurant, his back against the window, a notebook and a glass of water in front of him. I like Joe. I'm meeting him today, in part, for that very reason. He's a nice American guy with a nice American set of flawless shiny teeth who has a balanced nutritious diet, a supportive family and a mixture of attractive friends. Because of his accordion-like mouth, every time he opens it he loses approximately seventy-four per cent of his face. Now I'm sitting across from Joe at a shaky table and his mouth is moving, because he's telling me he has become a 'life coach'.

'It's about setting goals and achieving them,' he says, as we sit in a cheap Mexican dive up on 9th Avenue in Manhattan, near all the other cheap Mexican dives up on 9th Avenue in Manhattan ... tequila and nacho dens lost among the Laundromats and grimy bodegas plagued by the scattered remnants of free newspapers.

'You make a list of the things you want to do, and we meet once a week, or twice a week – or over the phone – to see if you're any closer to fulfilling them.'

Then he takes a sip of Coke. My friend, it seems, had turned into a human self-help book.

Earlier that morning, before the meeting, I did my research. Meaning: I Googled. A life coach is considered – usually by the coach himself – to be an expert in 'self-actualization', a creature designed specifically to aid you in attaining contentment, personal fulfilment and lots of money. All of this, I'm thinking, leads to that elusive place called happiness. I can tell it's working for Joe, because he's happy telling me about it. Now he's telling me about 'assessing negative behaviours', the kind that create 'obstacles for success'.

I try not to drink during the day – I'm thinking it's got to be one of those obstacles for success – but, here, looking out of the window, absorbing the background noise that is Joe's chatter, I decide it's time for a margarita. Although I really like Joe, I don't like sitting on a wobbly chair with stale nachos and watery salsa in front of me being told that my life needs fixing. I know Joe means well, but I want to throw him into the river. He can clearly tell I'm a miserable little man, a perfect inaugural client for his fledgling business.

I guess I'm miserable because of work, where I can see the end of my noisy career looming. My contract for my overpaid position in magazine publishing is coming up in a month and my interest in continuing there has already evaporated. I have a dream job, I suppose – working on a magazine whose primary focus is Carmen Electra's breasts and beer. If you lose interest in that, you know something is wrong.

Joe is the second or third life coach I've run into but, sadly, not over. It seems an occupation born out of a mishmash of 'light' disciplines – the kind of stuff a young American might have majored in at college in order to avoid getting up before noon. Thing is, everyone believes in this crap now. Well, at least in America. Or to be more precise: New York, and the parts of California where people still drink their own urine.

Joe talks some more, and smiles a lot. To his credit, he can talk and smile simultaneously – and sometimes, oddly, when he is frowning he is also smiling. He smiles even when he bites his nails. He's doing it right now, and I wonder if he knows he's doing it. I see a rat trundle down a stairwell, oblivious to my current state.

The meeting feels like it's ending … Joe has done his pitch, and I've sunk a pitcher of booze. Still I have no real idea what he will be doing to improve my life, but I do know this: It will cost me $500 a month to let him try. And in a fairly quick surrender I agree to be his guinea pig, and this makes Joe smile even more.

My new regime as a life coach client lasts briefly. I make a list of things to accomplish … and I stop right there. My motivation wanes. I am a dismal failure and I can't blame Joe for that. He approached me because I was an easy mark. He could tell I was unhappy. I didn't know how unhappy, but I suppose anyone could see it in the tired lines on my face. My life in New York had run its natural course. I had done all the drugs, drank all the booze, screwed all the women, yelled at all the cabbies and kicked all the rats along 43rd Street. I had used all of Manhattan up. And vice versa.

I quietly break up with Joe over the phone.

'This isn't working out,' I say, 'but I really appreciate all the work you've done for me.'

His voice cracks as he says, 'That's great, Greg.' And it seems for a moment that some of my misery has rubbed off on him. This is the first time in a while I actually feel good – so maybe there is something to this life-coaching thing after all.

The following day I run into a colleague – a pleasant friend whose mood is consistently modulated by fun-sounding antidepressants. Without asking him, he makes a suggestion: 'You should see this guy – he's like a nice uncle,' he says, handing me a phone number for his shrink. I must be wearing a sign that reads, 'Hates life. Please help'.

I am sitting on the couch now, trying my best to appear interesting. I'm telling the psychologist bits and pieces about my life and he seems engaged, which he is paid to be. He's nodding. But for a moment I believe his eyes may have closed. And then his phone rings. He rouses himself to answer it, while I'm still talking. I peer over to his notebook to see what he's been writing about me, but all I see is a dark circle in the upper-left-hand corner. My life story so far has forced him to doodle a black hole. In this single hour session I have not learned much, except that the doctor's son is going to be late for dinner.

I don't blame the doc. My concerns, complaints and lame jokes are mundane and probably no different from those of any of the other countless millions of men mulling about the Manhattan grid. The only difference is I am probably shorter. So, one life coach and a shrink later, life still sucks. I have paid two men hundreds of dollars to make me happy, and neither of them removed their clothes.

I leave his office, never to return. I head to the gym in my building and perform forty-five minutes of repetitive stepping exercises on a droning, lumbering stair climber. Next to me, another man is doing exactly the same thing. On the other side, ditto. The good news is, on that stair climber I begin to realize where my unhappiness might be coming from. Constantly moving forward, seemingly on the way up and never stopping, I am heading absolutely nowhere.

Forget the stair climber, it's happiness, I think, that's making me unhappy. Or rather, the thought of happiness, the pursuit of happiness, and those who claim to possess the tools to find happiness — all this happiness baloney is making me unhappy. Happiness is a myth but, worse than that, it's one I keep believing to be true. I am a thirty-nine-year-old man still believing in Santa Claus. Worse, I am wearing Lycra and I'm on a stair climber, which makes it hard to have a claim to any existential dilemma.

2. THE LETTER 'U'

Later, leaning on the windowsill of my stifling apartment, thirty-four floors up, I stare down at the belching orifice that is the Lincoln Tunnel. From my window, every day, I watch the cars stacking up to get in. Even as high up as I am, I can taste the exhaust. I need to get the hell out of here. For a moment, I entertain the idea of Australia. I've been there once, and have fond memories. Outside a bar in the Hunter Valley, around midnight, I punched a wallaby. It remains the most gratifying experience of my life.

But then I think to myself: Australia. There are Australians there. I scratch Australia off the list.

A day or so later I get a call from a friend in London, informing me that a job has opened up at a struggling men's magazine: 'You up for it?' he asks.

I have been to London two or three times before – just for business, and never long enough to learn anything useful – but I enjoyed England the way a tourist would enjoy it: I walked around in khaki shorts and sandals and drank a lot. I tried to pick up British girls, but failed miserably. I believe I might have thrown up once or twice in a hedge. Those are my favorite memories. Or rather, 'favourite', as it's spelled in England. It's that extra 'u' that makes me warm up even more to the idea of moving. There are no 'u's placed in American words, unless we need them. We stockpile them in a converted military bunker in Nebraska.

In England, it seems that 'u's are regularly inserted into words, sometimes uuuunnecessarily. Why all these superfluous 'u's? I'd like to think it's because England cares about 'you'. Or more importantly, me.

But what do I know? On my trips to England, I spent most of my time hiding in apartments and eating sandwiches. In the US, most of the stuff I've heard about England is pretty bad, usually told to me by people who happen to be English and are now living among New Yorkers. They tell me that:

- the food is terrible
- the women are ugly
- the health care is atrocious
- the beaches are polluted
- the dentists are incompetent
- the cabbies are racist
- the taxes are abysmal
- the drunks are violent
- the children carry weapons
- the weather is relentlessly depressing
- there are too many 'u's in words.

I know it can't be all that bad. Ugly women? Bad food? Violent drunks? You just described a wedding reception in New Jersey. I've seen it.

In order to get the job, however, I must gain approval from the owner of the company. Without ever actually talking to me, he gives me the nod. I get a call from a British man named Bruce, and the deal is done. All I need to do is talk to real live Brits to find out if I can survive in a place where people wear black socks in the gym.

The overwhelming consensus from my survey of every Brit I know is to go.

'You'll have a blast, mate,' they say, right before patting me on the shoulder and then returning to the game on the 'telly'. I am convincing myself, too, that it's time to move on.

So, after much thought, I make up my mind. Or maybe my mind gets made up for me. Either way, I'm off to London. I tell my friends and family, and shut off my cable and electricity. I find a creepy guy to sublet my apartment. I throw out the ketchup in my refrigerator. It's been there for five years. It still tastes fine to me, but sometimes you just have to let go.

3. ZIPPERS

It's time to move. But the big problem with moving isn't packing. The big problem with packing is moving. I love packing. I hate moving. Packing is fun because I like opening and closing things, as long as zippers are involved. I love the sound of zippers. I own about a dozen zippered bags. Inside those zippered bags, I often keep other, smaller zippered bags. My favourite zipper at the moment is on a bottom-separating sleeping bag that comes with a reversible (two-handled) slide. I don't even go camping, but you can't find a better sound than a sleeping bag being zipped up. When someone inside that sleeping bag is a barely conscious and panicky Crater Lake National Park Ranger – well, that plays like an orchestra to my ears. (You can never have too many sleeping bags: I have six.)

What kinds of sounds might I expect in London? Who knows? Great sounds, I'm sure. I am also certain, however, that whatever sounds they are, they will all be preferable to the one I hear as I stand in my apartment hallway, dropping dozens of porn DVDs down the garbage chute.

4. RULA LENSKA

After giving away my furniture and stuffing all my clothes into five gym bags, I'm at JFK airport. I've checked my bags, and I'm heading down those flimsy hallways to board the plane, where I am greeted by a friendly British flight attendant. She is attractive and older – in an attractive, older way. I want her to comfort me, read me a story, scratch my feet.

It strikes me that many older British women resemble ageing male rock stars, and vice versa. Look at Mick Jagger – he would make an ideal, sexy British grandmother. David Bowie would be a great 'mum' if you came down with a cold. He would bring you tea and biscuits. He would probably be wearing a two-tone silk kimono robe with patch pockets, with an inner tie closure with a loosened belt . . . no shorts underneath.

Back to the attendant: she has that wiry doll hair you always see on women in old Hitchcock movies. And on antique dolls. I want to gently comb it from the base of her head, wet it in cool soapy water, work my fingers through it and rinse thoroughly. Then I will untangle it, using thickening conditioner, and comb it. Not with a human brush – they carry oils that collect dirt and grime. I will probably use one of those doll brushes with the soft bristles. In the end, her hair will be very shiny, and I will be in prison (probably Belmarsh, which I hear is nice).

What is going on inside me? Where do these feelings come from? Is this a new aspect to my psyche – this unnatural and growing attraction to older British women – or is it simply a reawakening of something long suppressed, over decades? Maybe it's based on 'repressed memories', born from repeated viewings of Julie Andrews in *The Sound of Music*.

British women: it's a combination of the voice and the accent that makes me weak, hopeless and glassy-eyed around them. It's what drives me wild now, and it's what drove me wild as a kid when I would hear Rula Lenska do those VO5 commercials in America. They made me tingle in all the bad places, usually when I was at the foot of my parents' bed. When British women speak, it's like being enveloped in a coat made of Andalusian foals.

They say events in childhood always influence your decisions later in life. I could say that it might have been those commercials that ultimately led to my coming to London thirty years later. As a young boy, seeing and hearing Ms Lenska I was confused, and later smitten. She was unknown in America, and this made her even more mysterious.

In a way, Rula became a symbol of Britain for me: exotic, remote, alluring, old-looking. I knew one day our paths would cross. Until then, I would simply write her disturbing letters on tissue paper. And then eat them.

On the rare occasion when I find myself talking on the phone with an older British woman in customer service (perhaps ordering biscuits abroad, or maybe a Ben Wa Passion Flower 18-inch vinyl rubber double dildo) I keep her on as long as possible; it's heroin for my ears.

In my early teens, a British woman in her mid-forties moved in at the top of our street in San Mateo, California. She had a delicate and engaging accent that made everything she said sound like soft rain rolling down a tin spout. I remember how I used to repeatedly beat up her young son, Simon, just so she would come over to gently admonish me. Sadly, I have no idea what happened to her. I do believe her son was eventually found hoarding human remains in a makeshift dungeon. I'm pretty certain I had nothing to do with that.

One time, I admit, my predilection for British female accents sent me skulking around the internet to satisfy my cravings. I found a recording made by a 'retired bus conductress'. It was recorded in 1999, and it lasted approximately five hours. During the recording, she talked about 'old colliery houses' and the pride people took in keeping their front gardens well manicured. It made my hair, and other parts, stand on end. Every time she said the word 'mews' I would feel faint. Runner-up: the elderly woman from Welwick, Yorkshire, discussing how to make white, brown and spiced bread. It lasted four hours, and afterwards I had to see a doctor. I told him I had 'leaned in against a stove and burned myself on the nickel plating'.

He didn't buy it for a second. No matter.

I know it's early days, but I have yet to meet a fat British woman. They are almost all tall, skinny or shapely. And their cheekbones are so, well, cheekboney. Perhaps it's because I only find myself among women who are travelling from cosmopolitan centres, and the squat, pale and pudgy females are to be found roaming the countryside, feeding on field voles.

The longer we fail to address this quandary, the longer this question will remain unanswered. And more field voles will die. Needlessly, I might add.

Did the flight attendant just wink at me? Or was that a twitch? Doesn't matter. I'll take what I can get.

I haven't even left the tarmac and I'm thinking things are looking up.

5. THE PLANE

I take drugs when I fly. For this reason: you can die when you fly. Or rather, I can die when I fly. If you're involved in a car accident, you usually live. In a plane crash, you die. There are no 'flat tyres' or 'bent bumpers' in a plane crash. If something goes wrong with a plane, hours later someone in a jumpsuit will be putting bite-sized pieces of you in a bag. No one asks for a contact number before you take a cab.

As for those so-called experts who say it's safer to fly, I wonder how many of them have since died in a plane crash.

Of course, they aren't talking.

My irrational fear of flying is based on a rational fear of death. Having grown up in the USA, I can't bear the thought of dying. I am simply too young and handsome to end up incinerated in a mid-air collision. Or have my body parts – after years of meticulous sculpting at the gym – recklessly scattered over a cornfield in Ohio. More importantly, in America there are just too many things I would miss if I were dead. Applebee's baby back ribs, for example. (I think it's the dark brown sugar they use in the sauce.) I also enjoy high-fiving.

In America, you're not supposed to die. In the same way that you're not supposed to lose your hair, become impotent or smoke. When you're flying it's just unacceptable that you may crash, especially when you've just got hair plugs, a Viagra - prescription and a nicotine patch slapped on your testicles. You probably think, as well, that an airline disaster is not pencilled into your calendar. Perhaps you can fit it in next week, Thursday, say, between eleven and twelve noon. By then you may have 'a window in your schedule'. I wonder if I'll still feel this way about life (and death) once I'm living in England.

Before the plane takes off I sit back and try to relax. There is a nice girl sitting one seat away, near the aisle. She smiles at me (her teeth are crooked) and I smile back. I hear her talk on her phone briefly, and she's British. She asks me to turn up the air-con dial above her head, and I gladly do so. I twist that dial swiftly, counter-clockwise, as usual. Thank God I exercise.

We talk for a bit. Fifteen minutes has gone by and she hasn't mentioned a boyfriend or, even better, a therapist. Calling that refreshing would be an understatement.

I suspect this is an edge British women have over their American counterparts, although it may be too soon to tell. I do know this from twenty-five bumpy years of experience: American women tell you everything about themselves within the first ten minutes of meeting you. And the 'everything' includes a lot of crap about therapy, with a few anecdotes about cats. In America, all women have therapists. And cats. In fact, some women have two therapists, using one to discuss her problems with the other. And they also have two cats, using one to discuss her problems with the other. If the therapist also has a cat, then an entire session can be devoted entirely to comparing wallet-sized cat photos.

I am convinced that people who show you wallet-sized photos of their cats do so as an unconscious warning to everyone that, within a couple of decades, they will be living alone in a faecal-encrusted bungalow surrounded by eighty-five cats as uniformed men boom the door.

Why does the typical American woman see a therapist? Often it's to undo the damage of their previous therapist. I am willing to guess that British women do not have much need for therapists. My guess is that women in the UK refuse to take self-fulfilment as seriously as American women. And so, by comparison, British women seem wholly happy with their imperfect lives. They seem certainly happier with their teeth, that's for sure.

But that's just a guess. And I'm guessing that guess isn't too far off. But even that's a guess too.

All this guessing is making me anxious, so it's time to take my pill. I bid the girl a 'goodbye for now' smile, pop a pill and, in a blink, it's six hours later and I wake up and find myself alone. The girl is gone, having moved to another seat. There's a faint, stale odour around me. I have wine all over my shirt, but I am still holding my glass in the air, as if I am making a toast to an imaginary bridegroom. I get up, and assorted particles of food roll off my torso on to the floor. When did I eat, I wonder? What did I eat? Why is the nun crying? I vaguely remember a family sitting behind me. They are still there, but the teenage girl refuses to make eye contact. Did I emotionally scar her for life?

6. THE GUARDSMAN BEAR

I've landed at Heathrow and I've promised myself I will buy my
dear mother a gift upon arrival. Heathrow Airport is vast, with
hallways that coil into each other like a large intestine, but one
filled with people instead of poop. Every time I make a turn from
one long hall into another, I expect to see Customs but I don't. I
see another hall. And more people. It makes for a lovely walk –
one that for me will invariably end up at Glorious Britain, the
shop.

In the US, we don't have 'God Damn it, America is Great!'
shops packed with baseballs, apple pies, and high-powered
rifles – which, speaking as a fan of all three, is an omission. Here,
Glorious Britain offers no guns, but they do have a plethora of
British-themed magnets, badges and pins, ceramics, snow globes,
shot glasses, shortbread, die-cast buses, jams, teas and my
favourite: Churchill's confectionery tin set.

America has turned its back on tin, instead rushing to embrace
'cooler' metals that all the younger folks are into, like bronze or
this 'steel' thing they're all on about.

Sure, I know that Glorious Britain, the store, is designed for
tourists. But aren't we all tourists, when it comes to Britain?
Aren't we all just passing through this 'glorious' country, which
is one of the oldest and most beautiful in the world? Aren't we all
a bit taken in by the magical charms of a land that offers so many
options for key rings?

One thing is for certain, I kind of am. And that alone should be
enough for you. But if it isn't, I think you need to go to Glorious
Britain and get yourself a Guardsman Bear for only £13. It comes
with a red velour jacket with epaulettes, black trousers, and a
bearskin helmet. Cut a hole in the back (I did).

7. THE MINICAB

Arriving at Heathrow introduces me to something that I might be doing often during my stay in London: standing in lines thick with mumbling, confused people. Did I say lines? I meant queues. I like the word 'queue' because, in order to spell it, you must first ask four vowels to stand in line behind a consonant. The word is an embarrassment of riches, vowel-wise.

And that must drive the vowels nuts. Because they are probably British. And being British means they will spend the entire time asking themselves (silently) why in hell they're waiting in line behind a consonant. They must be in the wrong queue! However, they won't leave the queue because, no matter how much 'queue doubt' they have, they'll never give up their place. It's true. Even for vowels.

The queue to get into London is very long and thick. This must be a testament to the attraction the city holds for so many people. Did I say people? I meant 'foreign people'. London truly is a melting pot – a giant bubbly stew of different nationalities, all dragging luggage made from cardboard boxes and old twine. It warms my heart to see so many unusual types of people from all over the world coming to London to experience life. And ending up driving minicabs.

I am looking for one now, outside of arrivals. Minicabs are cheaper than black cabs, as I was told by a Brit on the plane, and 'they'll get you there in one piece'. That's an expectation I can get behind. As I pile my bags on to the cart and exit to face the large mass of people waiting for relatives, friends, I see many dark-skinned men wandering around holding cards with names scribbled on them. Off to the left, by the information booth, some guy has fainted. He's drawn a crowd, including all the hired cabs with their little signs. They are all standing in a circle around the body, staring down, still holding their placards.

One man without a sign approaches me and offers me a ride. He has a pleasant face, and he's dressed neatly – a light shirt tucked into dark trousers. I ask him how much, and he says forty-five pounds. He smells like he's been working all day and has tried to cover it up by having sex with a scented candle.

He speeds me into the city and the experience jars me, for the simple reason that he's sitting in the wrong seat. For an American who is used to the driver sitting on the left-hand side, I have to continually remind myself, sitting in the backseat, that the car is not driver-less.

I keep noticing that almost all the cars on the road are driven by women. As I look closer, I realize the women are simply sitting in the passenger seat. Whew, that's a relief!

As he makes turns from right lanes into other right lanes on perpendicular roads across circular turn-offs, my sense of direction and self is crumbling. I choose to stare at the back of the empty seat and listen to the driver pepper me with questions like, 'How long you here?', 'Why you here?' and 'Is that your hand?'

The driver exudes happy enthusiasm. He talks fast but articulately, and every response I manage is greeted with a 'very good!' or the more succinct 'Yes!' He is thrilled to be driving me in this country, because he's from somewhere else too – Afghanistan, I think – and he's charming me purely by being charmed himself. I've never had a cab driver like this in America, ever. He seems almost reverential towards having the opportunity to drive. In America, you never know if the cab driver is even aware he is in America. Or actually driving. Meanwhile, as we approach the city, the streets narrow and the scenery turns to betting shops and cafes. I feel a little optimistic. We pull to the side of the road, and the driver wishes me well.

This has never happened to me in America, either.

8. A BRITISH HOTEL

After I gather my bags, I struggle up the steps of a hotel in the heart of London's West End, on Bolsover Street.

Apparently all of its original features have been restored, from its ornate cornices to its stained windows. I marvel at the wooden panelling, the marble and granite in the bar. I also marvel at the Japanese businessmen milling about the lobby. There are perhaps half a dozen of them and they seem very excited, although there's never been a time when I've seen a Japanese businessman who wasn't excited about something. I salute their lack of ambivalence. To them, everything is Godzilla.

This hotel is home to the world's slowest elevator. Shiny and barely moving, it's the Steven Hawking of the transit set. The elevators are made of glass, which strikes me as funny because the short trip doesn't offer much in the way of views. I look around and see nothing, except for Japanese men looking up at me, and pointing.

The hallways are unusual here. They are chopped up by many doors, some that block the pathways for no apparent reason. I find this confusing. When I stayed at a hotel in Soho a few years back, I noticed the same thing. Narrow hallways separated by door, after door, after door. Then, here comes another door. Usually followed by another door (and some stairs).

The extra doors make it hard for me to remember where I'm going. I find myself wandering down halls I have no business wandering down, and I think I have discovered the kitchen, a pantry, a laundry closet and a playroom for bondage enthusiasts.

I am currently somewhere on the third floor, or maybe it's the third and a half, because I believe I went down a mini-flight of stairs. I suppose I should do some research on this penchant for excessive 'dooring', but I'd prefer to espouse a theory. Submarines have spaces inside them that are filled with air, and that allows the vessel to float. But in order to sink, the submarine needs to take on water in special chambers until the vessel is denser than the water around it. When the submarine needs to return to the surface, it simply lets the water out. For this reason, and on account of all the rain, I believe that London buildings were originally designed for underwater living, and in fact many hotels were conceived mainly as architecturally elegant submarines.

Like the elevator, the hallways and the old people wandering them, my hotel room is narrow and small. It's also decorated like my grandmother's house: lots of quilted pillows and lacquered furniture. The duvet – what Yanks call a 'comforter' – is a bright, puffy red thing. This one does not seem comforting at all. In fact, it looks as if it could repel bullets.

The television is teetering on the edge of a dresser. I expect to find a set of teeth floating in the glass by the clock radio, and I'm a bit sad that I don't. I drop my keys and spare change on the dresser and take a look at the amenities. There is a tea- and coffee-maker. I don't know how to use it so I turn on the television instead. There are people on it. Unlike people on American television, they are not beautiful. They have things all over their faces . . . pimples and wrinkles. They are sitting in a Laundromat. A frail old woman in a uniform is drinking tea and chain-smoking, her cigarette dangling ash from its end as she prattles on in a raspy voice. She is talking to a greasy-haired teen who has a big sore on his upper lip. I watch the programme for about ten minutes and, during that time, not a single thing explodes. I also do not learn a single lesson about life, and how to improve my own. This is not American television.

Then I hear this strange music and I am informed I have been watching *EastEnders*. I don't know what an 'EastEnder' is, but I don't want the show to end. Is it a portal into a parallel universe where normal-looking people drink tea in a Laundromat? Is it CCTV footage of the people who live across the street who drink tea in a Laundromat? Have I accidentally booked into a room used for police surveillance? I don't know the answers to these questions. But I do know this: I want to drink tea in a Laundromat.

9. BLOOD PUDDING

My cell phone rings, and it's Kerin. He's downstairs, outside, waiting for me. Kerin is managing director of the company I am about to work for, and he's a hundred per cent British. He's the most British person I've ever met, even more so than Dick Van Dyke in *Chitty Chitty Bang Bang*. He's what you folks call 'posh'. I've heard this word used only occasionally in the States, employed to describe Bentleys and vacation homes. In England it's used more broadly, to describe something upper class, fashionable or worth punching. It's also the name of a Spice Girl, the bony one that looks like a cricket in sunglasses. And, I'm told, Kerin has a 'posh accent' – which means 'incomprehensible'. He doesn't talk so much as smother words with a pillow. He can make 'bath' and 'chance' rhyme. Plus, he has an umbrella with him at all times. He likes to twirl it when he walks.

Outside we shake hands, and I notice he is dressed very smartly for a Saturday. He's wearing a blue blazer, a nice dress shirt and a handkerchief folded into his breast pocket. He's roughly seven years younger than me but, with the exception of his long, curly blond hair, he could easily be ten years older, at least in the manner in which he carries himself.

'You'll need this,' he says, handing me a thick book of street maps. 'It's the A to Zed, and it's mine but you can borrow it, if you like.'

Kerin can tell I'm confused.

'Zed. That's a "Zee".'

Kerin decides he wants to show me his apartment, or 'flat', so we grab a black cab and head to Paddington. When we walk into his apartment, to his surprise there are three stacked boxes. On top of them rests an envelope. He removes the letter from it, and realizes it's been torn carefully and neatly into eight squares.

'Bloody hell. This is the condolence letter I wrote to my girl-friend this morning. I just broke up with her. These are her things.' He points to the boxes. We open them and find every gift Kerin has ever given to her ('apart from the jewellery, of course,' he notes) along with a dirty toothbrush, old magazines, boxer shorts and half-empty bottles of shampoo.

'I can't believe she tore up the letter,' he says. He pieces it back together and reads it again, then places the remnants into his pocket. And then he asks the fateful question: 'Do you know what black pudding is?'

I say no, and Kerin smiles. 'I know just the place.'

We walk from his flat, in the direction of Hyde Park, along by the Serpentine Lake and past all the Arabs in their burkhas, sunning themselves on deckchairs, having picnics, surrounded by Harrods shopping bags. This might be the strangest thing I've seen in London so far, but I suppose they're not allowed thongs.

We stroll by the Serpentine, where Kerin points out the ducks, geese and swans.

'Swans will break your arm, Greg,' he says in all seriousness, before articulating a small history of *Peter Pan*, which is edified with a statue somewhere on the shore.

In-line skaters glide past, and I resist the urge to trip them up. As we pass the Diana memorial, I try to get out a question about it, but Kerin interrupts.

'I can't believe she tore up the letter.'

Along the way, Kerin points out all sorts of things.

'That's a stink pipe, Greg,' he says, stopping at what I now know is a stink pipe. 'These were used in Victorian times to carry the smell above the street. Everything smelled so awful that when the Victorians had enough money they paid a man called Joseph Bazalgette to build the sewer network, as cholera and effluence was such a problem. The stink pipes were ornate pieces of Victorian street furniture that wafted the crap out of your gentlemen's nostrils.'

I stare at the pipe.

'Just as a piece of trivia, Greg, Bazalgette's great-grandson is the producer of *Big Brother* in the UK. Do you think we can draw an analogy with the sewer?'

He walks a bit further, and murmurs, 'I can't believe she tore up the letter.'

When we drift towards Hyde Park Corner, Kerin points out No.1 London, the stately home where the Duke of Wellington lived, and the big arch in the middle. For a Yank, it means nothing but sounds impressive – more my fault than England's; there's just too much history and not enough brain in my skull to deal with it. But that does not stop Kerin, who stops in front of a mailbox.

'This is a pillar box, Greg,' he says, launching into a detailed history of these free-standing red boxes. 'They've been around for about one hundred and fifty years,' he adds, twirling his umbrella. 'I'm told this is where Sherlock Holmes would drop off his post, if he had existed.'

Thankfully, it's been about twenty minutes since he last mentioned the letter, and we end up at the back wall of Buckingham Palace, which we follow down through Green Park, and then into the front of the palace where Pall Mall starts. We have a look at the Victoria fountain, and then swing into St James's Park by the water features and down to the Inn on the Park, a pub next to Horse Guards Parade, where I could see the changing of the guard, if I felt like it. I am weak with hunger, and could eat anything – which I guess has been Kerin's strategy all along.

We grab a table and, after scanning the menu, I order the full breakfast, as Kerin suggests, because it has black (or blood) pudding.

'Black pudding is sausage, but it's really just cooked pigs' blood,' he says. 'It might have oatmeal in it.' Then he pauses. 'Bloody hell. I can't believe she tore up the letter.'

The meal arrives promptly, these two dark discs nestled next to a mountain of beans, toast, mushrooms and ham. I stick a fork in the black puck and chew. Kerin seems to be studying my face, waiting for me to spit it out so he can have a laugh. At first, my taste buds are disoriented, then rewarded – the equivalent of your eyes seeing porn for the first time. I broadly smile. I think I've fallen in love.

'This is awesome,' I say. And wolf it down. Kerin seems disappointed – he had hoped to disgust me. I eat mine, and his. It looks like crap, and probably should be illegal, but damn it's good!

Kerin whips out his cigarettes, and suddenly I beam with the realization that I can smoke in a restaurant. Pigs' blood and cigarettes. It doesn't get any better than this. Kerin looks me straight in the eye.

'Bloody hell, I can't believe she tore up the letter.'

After many pints at half a dozen pubs, we find ourselves at the flimsy Millennium Bridge.

'This was named after a Robbie Williams song,' Kerin tells me.

My legs begin to ache. We wander back to a main road, teeming with traffic. A double-decker, open-topped bus rumbles past.

'Hey, Kerin!' We look up, and there's a man on top holding a microphone. He's waving at Kerin. Kerin waves back. 'Who's that?' I ask.

'Tony Blair, Greg.'

10. GUINNESS

I've taken a nap and it's evening time. I decide to go for a long walk, alone, into town, which for me means walking in a straight line in a single direction. That way it's impossible to get lost. As long as I don't have to turn corners at right angles, I'm OK. I can't even draw a swastika. Too many turns. For that reason alone I would have been a lousy Nazi.

After ten or fifteen minutes I end up in a square-shaped area called Leicester Square. It's filled with people holding maps. I notice a lot of young women wandering around with backpacks, pointing at things with their soft, pointy fingers. Why do girls with backpacks always seem so tempting? I think it's because if a week goes by and no one has heard from them, it's OK.

Tourists pack the area, holding unfolded maps and doing their best to remain as obtrusive as possible. There are people holding clipboards, and others begging for change. But it's all very safe and I am feeling comfortable; and so I know, at this point, it's time to drink.

I look around for a pub and I can see there are a few. I head to the biggest one with a green awning and find a seat at a table, wait for the waitress, and call my mom.

'I'm here in Lie-kester square,' I say, and the men in football jerseys at the table across from me laugh. Hey, I had no choice. I smile to myself, and decide that it would be better to say as little as possible for the next two years.

This is what we Americans do when we come to England. Being louder and unfamiliar with how things are pronounced, we become neon signs for our unbridled naivety. And when we become aware that people find this funny, this makes us self-conscious. Eventually, it makes us homicidal. But at this point, I still feel only self-conscious. I bury myself in the menu.

I wait patiently for a waitress to come. I tap the table. I am beginning to wonder if they're paid to ignore Americans. I decide to go up to the bar and order a beer for myself. I elbow my way there and position myself in front of the taps. The bartender is pouring a Guinness. Then he stops, and lets the foamy liquid settle. I've not drunk Guinness before, and I've never seen it poured so gently. As I gaze longingly at the steel tap and watch the foam resting on the surface of that pure black gold, I want one.

'I'll have a Guinness,' I shout, waving my money and snapping my finger toward the other, female, bartender.

'In a minute,' she says. She heads off towards the opposite side of the bar and waits on someone else. Hmm. I wait a few more minutes. Then she returns, smiles shyly, and asks, 'Visiting?'

An American! Or possibly a Canadian. Canadians are a lot like Americans but with cheaper backpacks. No, she's definitely an American. She just said 'totally' twice in the same sentence. I can't leave now. I have to stay and admit that, although I'm thirty-nine years old and a fully grown male (in most places) I am nervous sitting here at the bar. I'm in a new country, I don't know anyone and I'm loud. I'm wary of approaching any Brits and speaking to them. I feel they are judging me. I hate being judged. Unless it's by a judge – and even when that happens I'm resentful.

An American bartender! If London were a deep and forbidding swimming pool, I have just found the edge at the deep end at which to cling. I talk to her nervously, but she moves away to help another customer, leaving me alone in mid-sentence (I was talking about cats). I light a cigarette and stare at the specials listed up on the wall.

Pudding? A bar that sells pudding? In America, only kids eat that, and usually it's for dessert, a kind of custard for very young people with unformed teeth. Pudding here can be many things. It can be made of suet, even blood. Who knows?

The bartender returns and so I order another pint. She stays this time, and I chat her ear off. I tell her everything: where I come from, why I came here, how long I've been here, and what I'll be doing while I'm here. I am pretty sure I don't leave anything out. I probably sound a little desperate. But she seems genuinely interested. I try to tip her, but she refuses. A heart of gold!

I have another pint, and then another, and then one more ordered from a male bartender with an Australian accent. When did he get out of jail?

Wanting to create an aura of mystery, I leave the Yankee bar-keep alone for a bit and turn my back so I am facing the tables full of people hovering over huddled pint glasses of ale. I love smelling smoke in a bar – it's been quite a while. I feel myself getting drunk. I stand up and feel, for the first time, fantastic. Then I shit my pants.

I choose not to sit down. Instead, I remove myself from the bar and shuffle past the tables of drinkers to the crowds outside. I walk north, back in the direction of my hotel. I carefully manoeuvre through the crowds on Oxford Street, waddling like a drugged penguin, being jostled by shopping bags and little kids. As I struggle towards Great Portland Street, I swear to never drink Guinness again. I swear to never go to that pub again and face that bartender who, judging from her expression, knew exactly what had just happened.

'Oh dear,' she probably thought. 'I hope he didn't get the chair.'

From now on I am drinking Stella in the bathtub.

The next day I tell Kerin about the accident. He tells me that you really haven't experienced the joys of being British until you've 'followed through' – a polite way of saying 'shat your pants'.

'There's a man I know who does this every time he drinks,' he tells me. 'That's when he knows it's time to go home and sleep.'

Kerin also goes on and on about 'having a poo', which to a Yank sounds like you're lunching with a German scatophile. We don't 'have' – we Americans 'take'. In the UK, I suppose that's just wrong. Where would you 'take' the shit to? A pub? A Broadway show? A Thames River 50-minute Circular Glass-Bottomed Boat Cruise, taking in all the sights from the majestic Houses of Parliament to the stunning dome of St Paul's Cathedral? I suppose not. It's probably not into architecture.

11. CUTLERY

After cleaning up and checking my messages at the hotel (there are none, not even from my mom, who I feel must know, in her mom DNA, about my little accident), I decide to investigate the restaurant off the lobby – a quiet bistro empty but for one married couple in their sixties. The dining experience is unaccompanied by the canned music one might find in a normal American restaurant, so I can faintly overhear the couple's hushed conversation.

'So that's what we'll do, then,' she says.

'Yes,' he replies.

There is a single roll of bread on a plate between them. Are they discussing plans to eat it?

I walk out and head a few blocks down the road to another restaurant, an Italian-looking joint with a lime-green awning. I peer in and see two waiters in bow ties milling about among the mostly empty tables. I am starving, so I push through the doors. The waiter seats me at a single table, facing the window. There's a fat man seated in the same direction on the opposite side. We are both facing the street, each with our own dinner roll. I suppose this is what happens to all lonely American men in London, on business.

I notice there are a few other couples in the restaurant, seated towards the back. I can hear their utensils hitting their plates, and I'm about two rooms away.

The wordless waiter brings me a steak and I cut into it immediately – the same way I always eat. I am a fast eater, gobbling meals so fast that I usually don't taste anything until the post-prandial burp. But there is something wrong with this steak. I chew as the acceptable method to break the meat into malleable pieces, but it seems the chewing only makes the beef more resistant. The more I chew, the more steak I seem to have in my mouth. I keep chewing for a few minutes until I use the napkin. I move to the boiled spring potatoes and the green beans. This is truly sadness on a plate.

The bill comes with a mint. The mint does not come in a

wrapper. It is round, and feels a little bit fuzzy. The meal costs £20, which comes to about six hundred US dollars. I wander out, thinking about McDonald's.

That steak I just had tasted odd, not like the steak I routinely enjoy in New York. I have no idea why. I can only say that it is different – almost as different as the manner in which it is eaten.

The first thing I notice when I watch the British eat is how odd they look using a knife and fork. Fork left, knife right – perhaps the most efficient method short of going no-hands. Brits hold their elbows almost parallel with the table, roughly six inches above the surface. I, however, rest my arms almost to my wrist on the table, allowing a relaxed posture as I pile protein into my pie-hole. From my perspective, Brits eat like giant grey kangaroos, with their little flipper arms never touching the table. When I point this out to Kerin later that evening over a pint, he explains that, 'We don't eat like fucking pigs.'

I agree. You eat like kangaroos.

Nonetheless, I decide at that moment to adopt this manner of eating, hoping to make myself appear more refined, and less like a pre-hominid. I have always eaten very fast, and it has always been an issue with fellow diners. Sometimes I eat so fast I don't even know what I'm eating. One morning after a particularly speedy evening meal, I found myself crapping out a small pot of silk floral flowers and floating, pastel-coloured votive candles. It was a wedding centrepiece. (I didn't even recall attending.)

I am especially impressed by the way the British eat peas. The following evening I watch Kerin do it, and it amazes me the manner in which he turns his fork over and rolls a line of them up the curve with his knife. It's a slow but graceful process, and one I would attempt, except I don't like peas. When I was younger, peas were the food that always ended up messing up your other food, floating into the peach cobbler in a frozen-food dinner. If peas were people, they'd be your in-laws.

I vow to eat much slower, so I can actually taste the food. Whether that is a good thing is debatable since, by and large, a lot of the food I have tried here, with the wonderful exception of blood pudding, tastes bland. But that's not the point. The point is to slow down and enjoy the company. And also to not choke to death. You can't choke to death if you eat slowly, and I've never heard of anyone choking to death on a pea. But I imagine, if you were Posh Spice, that could be possible. It would be interesting to test that hypothesis.

12. THE KING AND QUEEN

New to the neighbourhood I decide to go for a walk. Which means: I walk until I happen upon a pub. The whole point of walking in London, it seems, is simply to find a place to drink. Continuing to walk after one has found a pub seems irrational – almost like continuing to look for your flat keys after you've already retrieved them.

The pub I find is a proper, traditional British pub called the King and Queen. A great pub, it is. What's a great pub? One that's nearby. One that has wood panelling, sombre carpeting, dim lights, a jukebox, and approximately four old men sitting in their respective corners, their slightly demented, infested dogs nearby. The barmaid should be fat but attractive – or what I call *fattractive*. A dartboard is mandatory; a drug dealer, optional. (There, I think I may have just described every pub in London.)

I like the King and Queen because it satisfies most of the above, and then some. There is no drug dealer, or at least I don't recognize him. The pub is damp and empty in the early afternoon, with old signs and dated photos of ancient football teams on walls made of dark panelling. I love dark panelling.

Why don't we panel more things? I think the world would be a better place if it was like a British pub and we panelled everything. I'm sure there are some people who would disagree with me, but we could simply panel over them. The rainforest would be of better use, I think, if it was made into panelling.

I prefer the beauty of the dark British panelling in pubs and bars over the imitations you'll find in New York, Boston or Chicago. Because they're just that: pale, sad imitations. If you want real, authentic wooden panelling, you have to come to London. Or perhaps to a store that sells real, authentic wood panelling.

I have noticed that all the London pubs I have walked by and peered into feature wood panelling that covers all or part of their walls. Sometimes the panelling is paired with another material on a single wall – it isn't unusual for the top of a wall to be drywall and the bottom half to be wood panelling or wainscoting.

'Wainscoting'. I like that word! It sounds like something you might do on a Saturday afternoon if the weather was pleasant. 'Darling, why don't we go wainscoting with the O'Connors?'

Why don't we, indeed.

Wood panelling is typically installed as solid, interlocking boards. When they interlock, they appear to be made of one single piece. I like this idea: all of these panels working together to make me feel calm and relaxed. It's like a forest, but better organized.

Panelling = tranquillity and relaxation

Lack of panelling = pain and sorrow

See any location where forests outnumber the panelling and you'll find nothing but tragedy and strife. Rwanda, Bosnia, Zimbabwe, Essex.

Along with panelling, I have discovered another advantage that British pubs have over American bars: they are dark. Really dark. Darker than the darkest part of a dark thing you find under your shoe in the dark.

I have seen the light. And it's dark. Literally. American bars are just too bright – which cancels out the whole point of going to a bar. UK pub managers seem to understand the most fundamental purpose of a pub: to offer escape from the flashlight of God also known as 'the sun'. For me, the sun is a constant reminder that it is daytime, and I should be doing constructive things to fill up that time, like feeding the homeless, or at least kicking them. I don't need that kind of guilt. Pub darkness, I realize just now, is a perfect atmosphere to escape the shame you feel for sitting in the darkness of a pub at two in the afternoon.

Another great thing: When I go to the King and Queen for a second time (which interrupts another 'walk'), the bar becomes my 'local', and I become a 'regular'. At the K&Q the bartender already knows my drink of choice, vodka and soda, and has it ready for me before I've placed my parasol on one of those handy hooks beneath the bar. Oddly, the soda comes in its own bottle, and the patron must pour it in himself. I suppose this is to make sure you know you aren't getting cheated on booze. Brits are serious boozers, and I can certainly drink to that.

The pub, for a grown man, is the closest he can get to that big warm fuzzy blanket he had when he was a little boy. Like that blanket, it's comforting, welcoming and smells of bodily fluids. (Speaking of which, an old man at the bar told me that in the good old days, men used to urinate right there into a gutter at the bottom of the bar. And frankly, a man who thinks pissing in public is part of the 'good old days' is a man after my own heart.)

This is yet another reason why so many Yanks go to therapists, and Brits don't. They go to the pub instead. Most of the people in the pub look genuinely relaxed, unencumbered by worry or heavy pressure. When I sit down, I begin to feel the same way, as all my stresses seem to float away during the middle of my third pint. I suppose, for many men, the pub must serve as the one-stop shop for mental realignment – a cognitive lube job as supplied by the pub manager, whose name is usually Mel. You go there to sit, think, chat, sip, sit, think, chat, sip. Before you know it, all your troubles are gone, as is your wallet, your scarf and flat keys. But if you're really lucky, you may find a glass eye on the floor that's yours to keep.

It will probably taste salty. Like a bar snack.

13. THE DISHWASHER

I have packed up and moved out of the hotel and am about to spend my first night in my new flat, which is a five-minute walk away. Oddly however, it took me fifteen minutes to get there, because I got lost. Twice. In London I can get lost by simply walking a hundred feet in any direction. It's true. Try it (not on a bridge).

The flat is exactly how I imagined it. Because I had seen photos of it on the internet. Thankfully, it has come already furnished. 'Furnished' is Latin for 'containing two short, blue sofas, pale wooden chairs and dining table, a bed, a vase full of plastic flowers, four generic paintings, a mirror, a glass coffee table and one mouse'. You could call the décor modern, but I prefer to call it 'an accountant lived here'.

At this point I should mention the washer/dryer combination. The few things I notice right away:

- It's in the kitchen. Who cleans their clothes in the kitchen? Not me. I certainly don't make soufflés in the laundry room.
- Back in America we have separate machines that do separate things: one for washing, and one for drying. Why would you decide to make a machine that does both? This is the mechanical equivalent of a sequential hermaphrodite – an organism that starts out as one sex, and changes into another. It's a downer for most parents and makes it nearly impossible to buy the appropriate clothing for school.
- The machine is actually small enough to fit inside my washer back home. In a sense I could wash this machine in my washing machine, if I so desired (and I do).
- My first wash that came out of the machine was more wrinkled than Michael Parkinson's ball sac. And probably as damp.
- I have now found that it's better just to wash stuff and leave it all over the flat to dry. I learn of this tactic while walking around the neighbourhood, peering into people's flats. Everyone seems to stretch out their wet clothes over any

surface they can find, whether it be a windowsill, radiator or snoozing member of the family. I now lay the clothing on top of everything. My flat looks like the set of one of those movies where humans are vaporized into powder and all that remains are the clothes. I think it was called *Love, Actually*.

The wall in the front room is crooked. How can a wall be crooked? But it is. At first I thought the paintings – bland scenic scapes probably purchased from a hotel chain – were hung wrong, making the wall just seem to appear crooked. But now I have come to believe that the paintings are fine and it's the wall that's a problem. How do you have a crooked wall?

And why are the floor panels bubbling up?

I can't change the light bulbs, because I can't unscrew the glass surrounding the bulb. I call a man to come in and do it for me. He does, with a look of friendly disgust, in about forty-five seconds.

I don't have a doorbell. Everyone else has a doorbell, but not me. I've asked about it twice, but now I'm letting it be. Not having a doorbell offers a great excuse when you need to hide from someone. Like, say, someone who comes by to install a doorbell.

Every time I shower I flood the bathroom. I don't understand why I don't have a real shower. This is a tub and a long hose I wrestle with to attach to a clamp. This saddens me, and soaks the bog roll.

There are two locks and I have a key for only one. So now I've locked myself out. I call Kerin and spend the night at his flat. When I get there the boxes of crap left by his ex are still there. Weirder, he has a tub in the middle of the bathroom. To clean myself, I stand in the tub and wrestle the spray nozzle around my body, unaware that as I spray my shoulders I also spray everything behind me. I drench nearly everything in the room – but it wasn't like he really needed that watch.

After some research (two hours), I find the only logical reason for my screwed-up flat is this: it is one of many that make up a building that used to be ITN, a television production company. ITN was apparently the first network to employ 'newscasters'. I can only believe that it is the ghost of champion athlete

Christopher Chataway, the first ITN newscaster, who is undermining my appliances.

The only hole in my theory is that Chataway is still alive. Ostensibly.

14. TRAFFIC WARDENS

My little neighbourhood is quite beautiful. Known as Fitzrovia, it's famous for many things. I've discovered that the embassy of Turkmenistan is just down the road, near a gay bondage store with blacked-out windows that I sometimes walk past when I'm not doing anything around midnight on a Sunday.

I live across from a delightful pub, and around the corner, another. If I do a zigzag at the corner of Wells Street and go up Riding House Street, I'll hit Great Titchfield Street, which is a cobbled carpet of delightful shops, many of which do not remain open longer than maybe three months. My favourite – a Japanese florist and cafe combination – had a going-out-of-business sale simultaneously with its grand opening. There is one clothing shop, fronted with mannequins in the kind of long flowing dresses worn by ageing actresses when they come to accept an 'achievement' award. I have yet to notice a single customer in the place. Maybe some rich husband bought his wife a store just to get her out of the house.

A local told me that this neighbourhood is called Fitzrovia because it was known for gatherings of writers and scholarly types at the Fitzroy Tavern. Fitzrovia is also home to the Telecom Tower, which looks like a giant vibrator.

'There used to be a rotating restaurant up there, mate,' a cab driver tells me. This has been pointed out to me many times. I usually make a joke that you should never get drunk in a revolving restaurant – the rotation of the structure cancels out the spin you get from drinking, leaving you completely sober. The driver usually nods and moves on to complain about immigrants.

Also called the BT Tower, its original purpose, apparently, was to transmit high-frequency radio waves all over town. Which explains, in part, why every time I walk by it I get a funny tingling sensation inside my skull. But the real purpose of the BT tower, I think, is to make sure idiots like me never get lost. Any time of night, wherever I am, all I have to do is look for the Tower, and I know I'm home. Whether I'm stumbling through

Marylebone, or staggering up the Euston Road, I can always find my bearings if I can see the BTT. It helps, of course, that I never stray more than four blocks from the Tower – and I almost never do.

Fitzrovia is a colourful place, home to many eccentric intellectuals and the London Foot Hospital. As well as the Royal Ear Hospital. Apparently the doctors in Fitzrovia cater only to sebaceous body parts, which must have thrilled Dr Harvey Hawley Crippen, who used to live around here. He was, like me, an American who had moved to London in the hopes of a prosperous future. But he also had a bushy moustache, killed his wife and chopped her to pieces, throwing her heart into a canal by Regent's Park.

I could never grow a moustache.

I am beginning to like this neighbourhood. And I'll tell you why. It's the streets. It's the simple but sturdy architecture. It's the simple but sturdy people. It all reminds me of one place that, as a child, I loved so much. Disneyland.

In fact, England – and London, primarily – feels closer to Disneyland than Disneyland does. True, both places feature idyllic village settings, their streets brimming with people. But for Yanks like me, England exists only as a facsimile of England; we see versions of it at country fairs, amusement parks or in movies starring Terry-Thomas. We know the country only by its charming imitations.

So I suppose visiting London itself is akin to visiting an authentic recreation of London. But with real junkies and wheelie bins. And creatures called 'traffic wardens'. In the States, we call them meter maids, but 'traffic warden' sounds much more impressive. They astound me with their powers of invisibility. They are nowhere in sight until someone parks up and then one seems to drop from the sky, pad in hand. In seconds a ticket is written and slapped on the windshield right before a man comes jogging out of a store to reason futilely with the warden.

The warden never looks up from the pad, and expresses no emotion, even as a man much larger than him is waving his fat fist at him. These wardens are almost always African, and emotionless. They do their job thanklessly, and over a few days of watching them, I come to admire how hard they work, given all the abuse they receive. I try to say hello sometimes, but they usually ignore me. I suppose, to them, when you're universally hated, human contact never amounts to anything positive. I imagine this is what it must feel like if you're French.

I quickly settle into my flat, and actually begin referring to it as 'my flat', rather than 'my apartment'. While I impress myself with my quick adoption of this new lingo, it sickens my friends back home. Still, I am acclimating, using pounds instead of dollars and buying curries instead of burgers. I have become friends with the nice gentleman who runs Olive's, the Indian restaurant on Cleveland Street. Every night I stop in to pick up my chicken tikka masala, and normally I am one of his only patrons. But perhaps that's because of the fact that the ratio of Indian restaurants in my area is one per person. I have no idea how these places stay open. My only guess is they're all just part of one giant Indian restaurant, connected by underground tunnels, pipes drawing food from huge singular vats of curry located in the centre of the earth.

Back home in my flat, eating curry off a glass coffee table, I feel alone, however. I wonder if I have made a mistake. And suddenly I feel like an untethered boat in the middle of the sea. And my stomach feels gross, and I feel things moving quickly down below. That's probably the masala. So I tell the traffic warden it's time for him to leave, and I go to bed.

15. THE LIFT

Today is my first day of my new job, and I am walking to my new office – a plain white building located in Cleveland Street, just a few blocks south from my flat. The streets of Fitzrovia are strangely quiet. The shops look empty and the streets are devoid of cars. I walk past a bricked-in schoolyard, outside of which is a red rubber ball. I toss it over the fence and head towards my destiny.

I enter through the glass doors of the square building, where I see the front reception desk, which is really a giant aquarium of exotic fish with a lady sitting behind it.

Kerin has told me, 'When the mags are doing well, the fish are happy and thriving.'

There are a few floating on the surface. Another is hiding in a castle.

The elevator is slow. In a British elevator, it seems, you truly experience living in the moment, because that moment seems to last for ever. Of course, American elevators are faster; they usually have further to travel and time is money. British elevators take their time, like British service. But both always seem to have mirrors inside, all equally successful in the properties of reflection. When I ride in them, I like to stare at myself and inspect my tongue. Any swelling or cobblestone-like bumps can mean trouble in other places. I have a very small tongue. However, watching television earlier, I noticed that celebrity chef Jamie Oliver has a gigantic tongue – one that's too big for his mouth. It's like a slip dragging from a car door. Look out for it next time he is on TV, whipping up a brisket, or whatever it is he does.

The most enjoyable thing about the elevators here – and what makes them far superior to those in America – is the recorded British accents. I love the way floors are announced using the recording of a female British voice. One that reminds me, again, of stage and screen star Rula Lenska.

Everything here reminds me of Rula.

The lift. That's what you Brits call it. In America, we call it an elevator. This is not a minor distinction – at least for me. The word 'lift' is simple, direct and explanatory: it describes the machine that 'lifts' you from one floor to another. In America, where everything is bigger, we prefer longer words to littler ones. Hence, why lift something when you can elevate it? What takes you one syllable to say, takes us three. Those extra syllables, you might say, give us a 'lift'. However, we might say it 'elevates' our mood.

If it's all the same to you, I get into the elevator, sharing it with two other people. No one says a word – a delightful departure from a typical elevator ride in New York, which usually guarantees hearing about a golf game or a goitre. Both are equally unappealing.

We wait patiently for the lift to find the targeted floor, which it inevitably does in a jarring, alarming thud. Maybe Brits appreciate the strained silences found in elevators if only as anticipation for the inevitable clunk. When it happens, you're just happy you're not dead.

I have never been in elevators with a maximum capacity of 'three rabbits', but lifts in London seem to be designed with that specification in mind. I like this: it makes you appear bigger than you really are – a nice effect if you're a short stocky person like myself. In England, a far smaller country than the US, I have grown simply by taking up more space. According to my calculations I am roughly five times the size I was in the US. And it feels pretty good.

16. JEREMY PAXMAN

I find my office space on the third floor, which is empty and quiet. Natasha, my pretty blonde assistant shows me to my gun-metal desk – the same colour as the sky and every bit as empty. The carpeting is torn underneath my chair and there are frayed cables coming up from the floor. A beer poster hangs crooked on the wall. Natasha offers me tea. I never drink tea, so I say no. She disappears anyway, and makes me tea.

I check out my desk chair, a black and grey contraption that adjusts in height by means of a lever under the seat. I sit down, and it quickly drops to the lowest level. I try to raise it back up, but it's stuck.

So I settle into my drab corner, my chin level with the desk surface. I begin to open and close the drawers. None of them seems to fit properly. The top drawer is full of unused ketchup and salt packets, probably 'a gift from the guy who had the job before me' I joke to Natasha, when she returns with tea. She informs me that the guy who had the job before me actually had an office with a door that opened and closed. He also had shelves, nice windows, bulletin boards and probably a foot bath.

I just have a desk. In a corner. And there is a strange smell coming from the bottom drawer. It's jammed, so I let it be. I survey the entire floor and walk among the desks, all of which will be manned by other employees I have yet to meet. I imagine they're all fairly young and good-looking – scrappy types in their mid-twenties who would not look out of place in a Lynx advert. I notice the beer fridge, fully stocked with Carling. A good sign.

I am now heading upstairs to the conference room to meet the entire staff and explain my role as their new boss. My goal, of course, is to energize them – to rally them behind me: a new editor from across the pond, here to turn the ship around.

I enter the room and find a dozen or so faces – sullen, unsmiling. It's very quiet. My new boss, Bruce, awkwardly introduces me to the staff, and hands me the floor. I begin with a joke. I wait for the laugh, but there is none. I look around the room and begin explaining my strategy for the future, which is never fun. I deliver my spiel, and feel nothing in return but smirking ambivalence. I am not even sure they're listening. I think I hear a giggle. Natasha is the only one nodding her head along with my suggestions but everyone else seems numb. It's as if the roles have been reversed, and I am there to impress *them*.

I go home that night, turn on the television and watch the news. I see this fellow, smirking as he conducts an interview. The interview subject is a politician, and he tries to make a joke. It's not a bad one, but it comes out feebly. The broadcaster, Jeremy Paxman, remains expressionless, then dismissive. I'm beginning to sense a trend. I wonder if this is how it's going to be all the time. The British cannot be impressed. Every man is this Paxman – sardonic, quietly mocking and, damn it, thinking he's smarter than you. And at that moment, I have a thought. The moment you try, the British sense that you're trying. And trying is . . . wrong. Not trying – that's the way to go, I tell myself. I vow not to give a fuck. It's one way to fit in, right?

17. THE PUB LUNCH

The next day, I wake early and start a fire in my kitchen. Yesterday I purchased what I'd believed to be a kettle in which to boil water for my coffee. I had actually bought a teapot. So I put water in the teapot, place it on the burner, and take a shower. When I return, the handle is on fire. This is the last time I make coffee.

I throw on my clothes, run a shaver across my face, gel my hair so it has that pointy look popular with meerkats and Brits in the media, and head out the door to work.

I live one block from work: 'over the road', as you Brits like to say. In America, we say 'across the street', which sounds much closer than it really is. To a Yank's ear, 'over the road' means an extremely long trek 'over' something, perhaps a road. And oftentimes, that's what it is. I have found that almost all directions I have received from Brits sound simpler and shorter than the reality of getting there.

'It's just up there,' says Bruce, as we walk from work one afternoon to an advertising call that turns out to be somewhere near King's Cross. I have found that the British have a different sense of distances and, for that reason, I usually have to assume they will be late for everything.

On the way to the office I stop and pick up some pens and pencils from the downstairs mailroom. I also get a container in which to hold the pens and pencils. It is round and made of plastic. It has a little reservoir for paper clips, but I don't get given any paper clips. In my old job, people were literally throwing paper clips at me. Here, no paper clips. I would go and talk to someone about this, but I don't want to make trouble so early. I meet two of the men who work in the mailroom. Both are huge. The paper clips will have to wait.

Back at my desk, I email my eighty-year-old mother. She lives in California, so it's about 5 a.m. her time, and she is probably asleep or playing internet poker. I look out the window, at the Middlesex Hospital. There are people standing in front of the dark old building, propped up on aluminium crutches, smoking cigarette after cigarette. It's raining. I start to experience a cold wave of regret.

But it dissipates as I meet Donna. That might not be her name, I can't remember, but Donna works as an assistant or something and, frankly, I'm not listening when she tells me because she is so unbelievably hot – although not in the way I am used to. Unlike American girls, she doesn't have straight teeth – in fact hers are graveyard crooked. She doesn't have the typical Yankee bod, sculpted by Stairmaster with an ass harder than asphalt. Instead it is curved in every appropriate direction. Here is a body naturally built, untainted by the bland hand of physical fitness. Her nose is bent. In America crooked noses don't make it past the age of sixteen, for every girl with one gets it fixed as a birthday gift from dad. Donna has everything wrong with her, by American standards, but to me she is drop-dead gorgeous.

We shake hands and she walks away. I stare at her for about an hour, and then it's already twelve noon and 'the lads' invite me to my first pub lunch.

In the US, editors who run big magazines are treated like celebrities. They get lots of expensive stuff for free, invitations to cool parties, easy access to top restaurants and exclusive bars, as well as junkets to faraway places where you can buy ten-year-old gymnasts named Liang for a dollar.

In the UK, it's different. Editors are treated like everyone else with crap jobs. Actually, they're treated worse. And we deserve it. Basically, all we do all day is sit at our desks surfing the internet, chatting on the phone and, when no one is looking, smelling our fingers.

Then around noon, we go to the pub for lunch.

In America, employees rarely go to lunch together. Moreover, the boss wouldn't think of eating with his underlings. And he certainly wouldn't get drunk as a goat with them in the middle of the day like I am about to do now.

Eight of us grab a big table at the King and Queen, and begin with a pint. Then we read the menu and go to the counter to give our order. One thing I love here: you order and pay at the same time here, eliminating the annoying steps that usually take for ever in American diners: requesting your bill, and then paying the bill, and then calculating the tip. This is time that could be better spent smoking, drinking and urinating on your shoes.

I order an English breakfast – a sloppy pile of eggs, meat and, of all things, beans. In America, we don't eat beans for breakfast, or even at lunch. Come to think of it, we don't really eat them at all. But finding a plate smothered with them in front of me makes me smile a little smile that means, 'Wow, that's a lot of beans.'

What's challenging about the pub lunch isn't the food, which I have learned may cause diarrhoea if you don't eat around the 'bad chip'. The real challenge is returning to work afterwards. If you're like me, you return in a haze of numbed drunkenness, with a head buzzing like a bag of wasps.

How do people do this every day? I'm ready to collapse. I realize now that the pub lunch is never really over after lunch is eaten. It pushes its influence into the late afternoon . . . then towards the evening, when I find myself at the same pub I had my lunch in, gulping 'lager tops' and then heaving said 'lager tops' into the toilet. My superiors would fire me, if they weren't next to me doing the same thing.

I can get used to this work ethic. I suppose there are similar competitive machinations at work here in London as there are in New York, but it is better camouflaged in the fog of inebriation. Meaning, we're all too drunk to try anything devious. I think, thanks to the pub, that none of us here really knows what we're doing. We really only fill in pockets of time around the pub lunch.

But I could be wrong. I often am, especially when I'm drunk. I'm too drunk now to work, but that's OK. Usually at work most of the time is spent thinking about doing work, thinking about ways of getting out of doing work, or emailing pictures of people doing horrible things to donkeys.

Right now, I toy with various objects around my desk. I have five containers of orange powdered drink mix, sitting on my windowsill. Most of it has hardened into gypsum rock. If I ever break my arm, I could make a cast from it. I also have a pen resembling a hot dog. And a case of 'Prevage' anti-ageing treatment gel. (Never put that stuff on your scrotum.)

18. CUNTS

I'm in my job barely a week when my boss Bruce informs me that
I have to attend an editorial conference taking place at a sunny
resort in Portugal called the Algarve. There, I have to make a
presentation to other editors, all foreign types with names ending
in vowels. I hate presentations but I've never been to Portugal. I'm
pretty sure it's in Mexico.

If you are unfamiliar with Portugal, or the Algarve, it's about a
three-hour flight from London. The airport there is small and has
a delightful gift shop that sells oversized pencils and undersized
notebooks with dolphins printed on them. The Algarve appears
to be one of those resorts that could appear just about anywhere –
Jamaica, Turkey, Cyprus – with its whitewashed walls, perfectly
maintained shrubs and pools, silent servants in matching uniforms, and buffets derived solely from an unspecified bird.

The point of the conference: to get all editors from the inter-
national editions to meet to discuss things that work at their
magazines. As far as we can tell, what works are tits. This makes
me want to shoot myself. In the tit. I've been in this situation
before – when you want to sell copies, show skin. It doesn't make
my mom proud of my work, and that kind of bugs me. I knew I
should have stuck to stripping.

Every editor is expected to reveal his own mistakes too, so we
all might learn from them. But one won't play: the French editor.
In fact, the very idea that we would even consider such a thing
makes him laugh. In French.

As an American, I have only seen antipathy toward the French
expressed by Americans. Our dislike of them is based mostly on
French characters we've seen in movies, almost always waiters.
Oh, and the war. But the Brits are far more creative in their derision of their cheese-fondling neighbours, advancing the notion
that every Frenchman should be shot. I admire this greatly. The
beauty of the French is their ability to unite everyone else in the
room against them. So, after a tense day of quiet anxiety, everyone
bonds under the single assumption that 'the French are cunts'.

Cunts. There's a word I've never said 'out loud' before until I came to England and hung out with the English. I am amazed by how easily it slips from the British tongue, and I suppose it might be their equivalent of the American insult 'dick'. In the US, a 'dick' is basically an asshole. In England, a cunt is basically an arsehole. So, algebraically, $A = B$, and $C = B$, then of course, $A = C$. Cunt equals dick.

But there's one exception here – when a Brit calls someone a cunt with genuine and sincere affection. I am willing to bet that only the British are able to pull this off. Over a beer, and for reasons I cannot remember, my boss Bruce says to me 'You are such a massive cunt' but with an inflection such that the meaning is unambiguously rendered, 'My dear friend, you are in many ways an impressive person and I admire you a great deal.'

I suppose this is a good illustration of the extremes of British reserve – to preserve the social fabric and avoid personal embarrassment you clothe naked sweet sentiment with the filthiest, whoriest word you can utter. So in certain circumstances it's actually polite to say 'cunt'. But I also imagine that if I tried to do it, it would stop any conversation in its tracks. So I'd better not.

19. MATES

Outside on the veranda of the hotel I sit with my new colleagues – Kerin, Bruce, Simon and Richard – drinking pints of lager and 'taking the piss' out of the French. I feel like one of the 'mates'.

'Taking the piss'. It took me a day or two to realize this doesn't have anything to do with urinating. In America, we simply 'take *a* piss'. Inserting 'the' for 'a' implies we are urinating into a container and wish to transport it somewhere. This might make sense if you were seeing a specialist and needed to 'take the piss' to get it analysed. I know now, of course, that 'taking the piss' means to make fun of someone, knock him down to size, or, as we Yanks say, 'joshing'.

'Hey man, I'm just joshing,' is what you might hear from an American college student, right before you hit him over the head with a bottle (full of piss).

I have 'mates'. And I've been here only a few weeks. This makes me feel warm all over. It surprises me, however, how many people consider me their mate. Bartenders. Labourers. Security guards. Bouncers at clubs telling me I'm not allowed in because I'm not on the list. Friendly strangers who want to sell me the *Big Issue*. Groups of youths trying to steal my sunglasses.

The realization hits: mates aren't friends. Mates can be anything. I learn this later, when accosted by a drunken man who keeps calling me 'mate' as he throws coins at my head. Mate can mean anything to anyone, and I've learned never to trust a man who says it too much. When a stranger at a bar keeps calling me mate, I put my wallet in my front pocket and hide my cigarettes.

British men possess a unique talent: by using 'mate' to combine friendliness with sheer menace, as though they're offering a moment of shared intimacy, and you might just let your guard down. And that's when they glass you. I've only seen this from villains in movies like *Trainspotting* and *Sexy Beast*, and it's scarier than any American bad guy from one of our mega-million blockbusters. Saying 'mate' to a stranger – that was probably the

main reason why the British were so good at invading and con-
quering foreign lands.

I know I have real UK mates here, however, right after the
other Americans show up. All of them have come dressed in
khakis, golf shirts and spotless penny loafers. They appear to
have been dressed by their moms. Meanwhile, British men seem
dressed like five-year-olds – shorts and T-shirts but with packs of
cigarettes clutched firmly in hand and a beer in the other. These
are seasoned five-year-olds.

Brits dress better than Yanks, despite the fact that Yanks try
harder. Maybe that's the point. I would not be surprised if before
this trip every American had gone out and bought a 'vacation
hat'.

I know I am not British. I am a Yank, but I work for the Brits;
and have no desire to talk to the Yanks. It's not that I don't want
to hear about their lawnmowers. Wait, yes – it's because I don't
want to hear about their lawnmowers.

After having a few pints at the hotel bar, I decide to take a nap,
shower, and then throw on a fresh set of clothes – a shirt and pair
of shorts that I will never ever be able to fit into again. And then,
outside my room, as I leave for the bar once again, I meet my wife.

20. THE UNDERDOG

Of course, she doesn't know she's going to be my wife, and neither does the good-looking man with her. But I do. I see her walking across the hotel pavilion, in close chat with said good-looking man. Both of them are very pretty – so attractive, in fact, that if they decided to spawn, their offspring would be a delightful puppy/kitten hybrid with a gooey chocolate centre.

Assuming they are husband and wife I ignore them. But as we walk past each other, the man speaks, employing an accent I recall from the 1983 film *Gorky Park*.

'Grek Gutfelt!'

I stop and the man approaches me. He is Sasha, a Russian editor, and Elena is his photo-editor. She has striking brown eyes and black hair resting comfortably on a model's physique. She is so out of my league, my left brain tells the right. She smiles, and I smile back. I look at her hands, and they are nice hands, there are no rings on those hands. They walk off. Sasha and Elena, that is.

I make my way to the bar, where I find the Brits. They sense something has happened to me. Something monumental. So I tell them, 'I've met my wife.'

They congratulate me.

This is not normal for me. I usually do not worry too much about beautiful women, precisely because I never go after any that would be out of my reach. I only hit on the receptive ones because it saves on rejection and/or getting beaten up by a larger, more handsome male who is temporarily in the toilet adjusting his thirteen-inch penis. Elena is simply something to wish for, while I look for something else more within my range. A dwarf, perhaps. With big tits.

But it is here in the Algarve, during this hot and stressful week under the white-hot sun of Portugal, that my ambivalence evaporates. For it's the first time I experience, intimately, Britain's passion for the underdog. I know I want this girl, but my new friends want me to get her too. And they won't let me forget it.

'There she is,' Kerin says, pointing over to her at the bar.

She's sitting across from a gentleman with the Italian publishing clique – men so perversely chiselled that even their cheekbones have cheekbones. This man possesses a mane of luxuriant hair and a twenty-seven-inch waist, resembling the most handsome pony I have ever seen. I want to strap on a Henri De Rivel suede seat saddle, probably in medium-brown 'oakbark' with removable handstraps and grained leather, and take him around the block.

Then shoot him, of course.

I sit at the bar, yards away, staring at Elena as the man buys her a drink. The Brits sit me down, and start buying me drinks. They offer support, advice and more alcohol – and they push me forward. They do this, of course, knowing I am clearly a hopeless case that will no doubt crash and burn.

For the next few days in Portugal I wander the grounds, desperately trying to get Elena to notice me. My attempts at conversation fall flat, every joke met with awkward silence. Her being Russian probably means she doesn't get my attempts at wit, but at least she knows I'm trying. The Brits find this funny, but they're still behind me.

I suppose I'm like a crappy football team, surrounded by supporters who know you're crap but root for you anyway. Their support never wanes, propelling me back to the bar to approach Elena, to say something even stupider than before. I always return, contemplate her silence, and start all over again. More shots, more encouragement, and more embarrassment.

And here's another lesson about British men. My new 'mates' come to my aid because they love a losing cause. If the losing cause wins, it's gigantic. If the losing cause loses, it's to be expected. You really can't fail with that kind of attitude to life, can you?

There could be a darker side to this enthusiasm for the underdog: sadism. Brits may love losers, but only if they can point them in the direction of defeat. This is what makes Brits especially friendly. They're extremely helpful when they know you aren't going anywhere better.

But, thanks in part to my newly found mates, I work up the nerve to ask Elena out on a date. She says yes, we exchange numbers, and I am a hero. Meanwhile, my competition – the gorgeous Italian guy – is now alone at the bar. It's OK. He won't go by himself. He has his hair.

21. CHICKEN AND STUFFING SANDWICHES

I'm back in London, and it's lunchtime. I love lunchtime! Most executives, I imagine, have a favourite restaurant they go to with other executive types. They sit and talk about their exciting lives over a grapefruit and jacamar salad with tofu and rau rum. If I was there, I might sample the local blue-fin tuna. But I'm not (I hate the colour blue). Instead I go alone to Sainsbury's, pick up some egg mayo spread and eat it with a plastic spoon in an empty corridor.

I can make a container of egg mayo spread last for two days. When I've eaten all of it, I save the containers and use them to make handy homemade crafts. For example, if you have to take pills every day, it helps to have a pill box to keep them organized, day by day. I should stop there.

I also like sandwiches. Years ago when I visited the UK I would purchase three or four sandwiches and eat them quietly in a dark room. I have often brought this up in conversations with Brits, and they are mystified. Apparently, Brits take these sandwiches for granted. Which is wrong. These sandwiches not only hold a special place in my heart, they have come to symbolize something I love about England: variety based on combining two basic ingredients that alone would be tragic, but, together . . . magical!

Right now, my favourite sandwiches are bacon and egg, bacon and tomato, sausage and egg, triple (Tesco) chicken and stuffing, egg and cress, and egg mayonnaise. The plastic packaging is adorable – the clear front allows you to inspect the contents just to make sure there isn't a thumb in it.

I like chicken and stuffing the most. It's a comforting meal, pre-chewed in texture and easy to swallow when you're in a hurry. You cannot find packaged delights like this in America because no one would think of combining chicken and stuffing together between two slices of bread. I eat it so fast it gives me hiccups. In the US, you can find drab affairs in vending machines, and there's the annoying fussiness of Pret A Manger's sandwiches, found all over Manhattan. But where's the charm?

It's near my desk, in my waste bin. There you'll always find something smelly. It's a sandwich or a sandwich remnant. Since moving here, I am weaning myself off a long-held fitness routine, and I am eating more sandwiches than ever before. I always buy more than I can eat, which is why leftovers end up festering in the bin. Where do I get my sandwiches? I get them from any one of the 12,345 sandwich shops located in a three-square-block radius. I pick the shop I want based on the colour hair I want to find in my egg mayo.

In the US, we don't have the vast number of quaint hole-in-the-wall sandwich huts that seem to dot the UK like blemishes on a cab driver's bottom. In the US, sandwiches are huge, sometimes bearing novelty names, usually based on dead celebrities or cheesy landmarks. They are all the size of infants. In the UK, sandwiches are dismal affairs: flat, slightly stale and brittle. Poorly made sandwiches are kind of heart-warming though – they were the kind your alcoholic mum made before she passed out in the hallway wearing only a compression girdle. Wow. Suddenly I'm hungry!

22. THE MORTIMER STREET CAFE

And when I'm hungry I get confused, because I never know where to eat. There are just too many sandwich cafes, and they are almost all exactly the same as each other. Thousands of identical, hole-in-the wall eateries all offering the same paninis, hard doughnuts in cellophane, Kit-Kats and warm Ribena, and, of course, jacket potatoes. Every glass shelf of every cafe is jammed with potatoes the size of van drivers' fists. With all these potatoes everywhere, I do not understand why the Brits aren't fat and the Irish aren't rich.

Because I live so close to work, I get up at 9:45 a.m. And each day I make it to work at ten on the dot, give or take thirty minutes. The time varies because of my erratic relationship with the neighbourhood cafe owners. When I moved here, the first cafe I went to was located on Mortimer Street, where I struck up a friendship with the guy who ran the place. He heard my accent, and asked where I was from. I told him, and he seemed delighted by the idea of an American living around the corner. I would see him on the street, and I would wave. He would wave back. He was a short dark man with a friendly smile, and his generosity often shone through when he would give me a free croissant with my coffee.

One day, I gave him a free calendar I had recently put out as a news-stand promotion, featuring a pile of half-naked women. He gave me a muffin in return. He never hung up the calendar, however. And I began to wonder if, perhaps, I might have violated some religious principle, and that maybe one morning I would wake up with a small American flag impaled in my chest.

It didn't matter, though, because a week later I stopped at a different cafe to pick up a sandwich. I struck up a friendship with that manager too. He was also a dark, friendly man with a friendly smile. We talked about the neighbourhood, and about my job. I believe he gave me an extra slice of turkey escalope in my sandwich.

Now I have two cafes to visit. This means that I have to ration out my trips to each. I will go to one three times a week, the other twice a week. Then the following week, I might flip the schedules – so, over the course of the month, I visit both eateries equally.

The problem, of course, is getting caught. This happened to me recently with pubs, when Mel, the manager of the King and Queen, wandered into the King's Arms and found me in the corner drinking a pint and smoking. He's never really looked at me in the same way again. I have been cheating on him. It's the same with cafes.

And now I've found another one, which has cheaper and better coffee than the others. And another that rustles up better breakfasts. And one with free newspapers. One doesn't have any ice. Another has Orangina. I don't know what to do. How do you break up with a cafe manager? Things are more complicated now I've found a tiny hole-in-the-wall shop called the Ship's Galley on Foley Street. The manager actually gave me a free soda. So I start going there more often.

This means I have to avoid walking in front of the other cafes, which has led me to taking different routes to work, adding minutes to my walk. This never happened to me in New York. In corner shops (we call them 'bodegas' in order to sound multicultural) friendships are never initiated, because no one desires friendship. Every owner is from Bhutan, Azerbaijan or Namibia, so we communicate by tossing weighted V-series professional throwing stars at each other. So you can be as rude as you like, to whomever you like, as long as you duck. Here I cross two roads I don't have to cross just so I'm not spotted.

In England, I'm paralysed by the infectious face-saving politeness that forces me to get more exercise than the postman. Maybe that makes me pathetic, but it's not so bad. I see more of the neighbourhood and burn off a few calories. If I continue at this rate, in a month I'll be circling down near Cardiff in order to get to my office. The bottom line: I don't want to hurt anyone's feelings. And that's a change of character for me. I used to be an asshole. Could I be turning British?

Christ, I just bought a scarf.

23. THE SCARF

I just bought my first scarf ever in the UK, at Selfridges for £38. It's black, with thin grey stripes. I named it 'Adair', which means 'exalted'. That, along with the purchase of a tea towel (which is actually a cloth used for drying dishes and has nothing whatsoever to do with tea), has almost made me a British citizen. In America, every person owns a car, possibly two. In the UK, every person owns a scarf, possibly twenty. By wearing a scarf, I have become instantly 432 per cent more stylish than before.

And more trustworthy. Scarves, for some reason, make you look like someone who 'cares'. In America, when I was at parties, no one trusted me to hold their babies. If anything, they kept their children away from me. But now that I wear scarves, people are literally hurling their infants at me. I credit the comforting and accessible look of the scarf.

People in the UK wear scarves because they know that keeping their necks warm helps prevent sickness. But the real reason for wearing scarves isn't because they keep you warm – it's because they make you look cool.

No matter what I'm wearing, a scarf makes me look better. I love scarves so much I actually bought another, smaller scarf, just for my scarf.

Scarves give off the illusion that I actually care about my appearance, and that I have a neck. I don't really have a neck. My head basically rests on my shoulder blades – the consequence of spending most of my life lifting weights and shrugging when people ask me questions about lifting weights.

Note to parents: discourage your children from lifting weights.

Sadly, since I moved here, I have also grown another chin, one that rests directly beneath the one I had since birth. I blame this chin on a lot of things, but blame doesn't make it go away. But a scarf does. Wrap it around my neck a few times and I instantly lose ten pounds off my face. That's what experts in the fashion business call 'style'.

Just a simple addition to my appearance – a scarf – makes it seem like I'm stylish. It's true. I could crawl out of bed, throw on a bin bag, some carrier bags for shoes, a basket made of animal fat for a hat . . . but if I add a scarf, I look fantastic. This is the secret to British fashion. It's not about being neat, or even looking as though you might have bathed a few times since 2006. It's about attention to detail. And that one detail is a scarf.

By wearing a scarf I have become so British that even Beefeaters ask me for directions. And by wearing scarves almost every day (even in warm weather) I am now eligible for all the normal benefits usually given only to people who are truly British. Meaning, more scarves.

It took me a while to actually learn to tie the right knot. Because of this, I initially lost two scarves. Their names were Chip and Duff, respectively. Finally, I learned to tie an Oblong. I learned by watching one of the 'chaps' at the magazine. His name is Joe Frost. Joe looks like a rock star, with his pointy blond hair, and he sings in a band using a delightful American accent. This confuses me, almost as much as how to tie a scarf around your neck so you don't lose it.

So I watched Joe. He doubled over the scarf then wrapped it around his neck. Next he brought the ends forward tightly. Then he opened the loop formed by the centre fold, and pulled the two ends down through the loop. Then he pulled the ends in opposite directions until the scarf fit as snugly as a diaper.

Or a 'nappy'. A nappy for his neck.

I love wearing scarves, and I won't leave home without one. Interestingly, in America if you wear a scarf you are assumed to be a homosexual, especially if you happen to be wearing the scarf while having sex with another man. In England it doesn't matter if a scarf makes you 'look gay', because most British men in the city 'look gay' already.

I feel bad for gay men in London, because you really have to act gay to stand out. British men dress so stylishly, with their low-slung jeans, perfect trainers, tight T-shirts and pointy waxed hair, it's sad to see gay men get lost in the mix. I believe this is why most gay Brits must overcompensate with campness, or their sexual identity loses cachet.

This assumption of gayness, represented by the scarf, is also why straight Brits get laid so much in the US. American women assume these little dandies are gay and invite them home to help them choose sofa patterns. Then those little dandies have horrible regretful sex with them. Bastards.

24. CRISPS

I am sitting with David Whitehouse on a park bench outside the King and Queen. David is a young 'lad' of about twenty-three. He dresses like all young men these days: penguin shirt, slightly baggy jeans, trainers. He has pointy hair, his face is unshaven, and his eyes are red. It's only one in the afternoon but he's on his sixth pint. I barely know him, but he grins at me and points over my shoulder to the street.

'Look at that, would ya?'

I turn around and there's a dirty-looking car, with a long cardboard box strapped to the bonnet of it.

'Shite funeral,' he adds.

That's enough for me, so I offer him a job on the magazine, and he starts working for me a few weeks later. To celebrate, he buys crisps, which in America we call chips – a word already used here to describe thin strips of fried potatoes. I hope you're keeping up.

I am appalled but strangely attracted to the flavours of crisps, which include prawn, beef and chicken. These flavours, by the way, are not fooling anyone. Does anyone purchase a bag of chicken-flavoured crisps and think for a moment that they are actually eating chicken? I would prefer that my crisps simply taste like crisps, not like some facsimile of another food I would actually order if I desired that particular flavour. If I want a beef steak, I will not eat beef-flavoured crisps. I will order a beef steak. Of course, the irony is, in the UK the steak won't taste like steak. It will probably taste like wood. Or wood chips, actually. There's a lesson in there somewhere, should you be inclined to learn it.

Another thing about crisps – Brits eat them differently. Or at least David does. When a bag is purchased, it doesn't matter who buys them, they're for everyone. And this is underlined by the method in which the bag is opened. David tears the bag down the seam on the rear of the bag, splaying it out flat so the crisps are available from all sides by anyone at a table. I've never seen people eat chips or crisps like this. Generally Yanks open then from the top, and pull from the inside. Only the purchaser can get at them. I suppose there's another lesson in there as well. But why fret over it? Dave has just thrown up in the toilet.

25. BANK HOLIDAYS

It's Friday afternoon before I realize I don't have to work on Monday. We're at the pub for lunch and the boys from work are talking about how completely trashed they are going to get this weekend. I ask why this one in particular, and one of them says, 'It's a Bank Holiday!' A Bank Holiday, they tell me, is a public holiday. They are called Bank Holidays because banks are closed on that day – which renders almost any other businesses incapable of remaining open. This seems like the strangest circular argument I've ever heard: the banks are closed because it's a holiday – and it's a holiday because the banks are closed.

The genius of this cannot be understated.

What's weird, however, is that no one at work has bothered to bring it up until now, on Friday. Apparently Bank Holidays happen at the same time every year but, in the days leading up to them, people act as if they've never heard of them. And once it dawns on everyone that they've got no work on Monday, the enthusiasm generated is frighteningly palpable, because it means more drinking!

'Hey, Monday's a Bank Holiday!'

'Is it?! Fucking brilliant!! I'm going to get right fuck-arsed!'

And to celebrate, everyone spends each Bank Holiday on a three-day bender. Maybe it's a way of breaking up the monotony of the grinding work routine. Or maybe it's because Brits will look for any excuse to drink.

Either way, not to be a party-pooper, I decide to do the same thing. For the next three days I go out and get drunk, at different pubs in the neighbourhood, and fall asleep by the early evening. If this is what a Bank Holiday is all about, I want more Bank Holidays.

26. IBIZA

Brits travel a lot more than Americans, mainly due to the fact that you're allowed more vacation days, and you're close to so many great places filled with foreigners you can throw up on.

Brits love their time off, and I love them for that. And soon, I will be going away for the first time in a while, for my fortieth birthday. I will be heading to a beach in Ibiza, or 'Ibeeetha', as you like to pronounce it. In the US we pronounce the 'z', which is a letter that seems invisible in the UK. I am still unsure what a 'zed' is, but I assume it's a shed for 'z's – hence 'zed'. (I await confirmation on this fact as we go to press.)

This tiny Spanish island is a popular destination, usually frequented by ecstasy-riddled Brits so messed up they think they're nineteen-year-old DJs when they're actually forty-two-year-old branch managers for HSBC.

It's now 10 September 2004, two days away from my fortieth birthday.

When some friends, Alan, Bill and Jack suggest I spend that day in the nightclubs and on the sandy beaches of Ibiza, I feel both excitement and panic. I know I am too old to have fun. Drugs are for young people who have nothing to lose. For me, now, I have everything to lose. I have a pretty good life and drugs – or ecstasy, which Ibiza is known for – scares the hell out of me. I don't want to overdose and end up in a foreign hospital, perhaps in a state of permanent retardation, my organs harvested for sick people who probably deserve them more than me anyway. (My organs would be no great shakes – particularly my uvula.)

Also, I should mention that things with Elena have been good. We've been dating for five months, and we are now engaged. It's not often I get the girl, and I surely don't want to fuck that up by being a monumental idiot.

For this reason I have to avoid the possibility of death. My death would ruin our upcoming engagement party, as I explain over and over to my 'mates' Jack and Bill, and Alan, who has flown in from the US. They reassure me that I will not die. That is enough for me.

On the plane with Bill, taking off from London, I sit amongst a group of UK holiday-goers and am instantly impressed by their relentless ability to inflict terror on anyone – a child, the elderly, a goat, or anything else that comes between them and a pint. Combining the refusal to sample other cultures with their inability to blend with the locals, the British traveller appears to be a happy antidote to the earnestness you find in the American tourist. They understand what travelling is all about: getting drunk in different places and explaining their public nudity to the local police.

The men surrounding me share a number of traits: they are drunk, loud, dressed in tank tops and track bottoms and hats, possessing barbed-wire tattoos around their biceps, and maybe another tattoo of the name of their favourite football team some-where else (this might be on a buttock cheek, so you won't see it until you are mooned, which most certainly happens about forty-five minutes into the flight). They are yelling at the flight attendants in a friendly, scary sort of way.

As I sit quietly amidst organized chaos, I begin thinking that a crash might be the only way to restore order. I call this the British drunk/disaster theory. It's only during a disaster that Brits sud-denly appear sober, while the rest of us are staggering around and screaming. I imagine you probably see this after major tragedies, or during war, in Britain.

To understand the difference between the modern British tourist and the average American traveller, here is a brief snippet of an American family queuing at security control at Heathrow:

Dad: 'I'm going to buy a magazine for the trip.'

Mom: 'We have to call the gardener when we get in to tell him to throw the newspapers over the fence so people don't know we're gone.'

Meanwhile a British couple sounds like this:

Man: 'Fancy a pint?'

Woman: *burp*

Wherever they are, Brits act like they own the airport. They buy their suntan lotion (never with any useful SPF number) and vacation drugs, and they're set. Then they head to the airport chain pub/wine bar and drink like it's last call, even if it's seven in the morning. Earlier, I sat at a bar at Heathrow and watched a middle-aged couple with bad tattoos drinking up until the very last minute of boarding. A delay would have driven an American family nuts; for the Brits it just means more drinking.

Unlike Americans, who always react anxiously to bad news, Brits usually see the glass half full. With rum. You must admire that. I do. I have learned so much from Brits, and I am not even in England. I'm in the sky, currently dodging beer cans from a man who looks like an inflatable version of himself. When we land, Bill and I grab a cab to the hotel and meet up with Jack and Alan. A man delivers a handful of pills. I take mine first. Bill takes his five minutes after me. Jack and Alan are already high as kites.

'It will hit you in about half an hour,' Alan promises me, so I sit quietly drinking a Corona waiting for 'it' to happen. I feel fine, sitting at the cafe table staring at all the beautiful people around me – shirtless, braless, and gorgeous – until one thought takes over my brain. 'I need to go to the hospital.'

I announce loudly: 'Take me to the hospital. Now.'

Bill tries to comfort me by massaging my neck.

'Greg, it will be fine. Relax.'

'No,' I say. 'Take me to the hospital.'

He keeps massaging, while Jack and Alan try to talk me down from my ledge in hell. Bill's hands feel like tentacles.

And then, like a plane landing above me, a crashing wave of cold air hits me and I am awash with mindless pleasure. Never before have I felt so ALIVE. I turn to Bill and say, 'My God, this is fantastic.'

Having taken his pill five minutes after me, he stares at me in ghostly horror.

'Take me to the hospital,' he says. 'Please . . . take me to the hospital.'

The rest of the trip is a strange contrast between what I think happened, and what really happened. In my head, I was truly alive – dancing on tables, swigging from champagne bottles, surrounded by beautiful women. I was living it up, living the dream. But two days later, when Alan shows me pictures of that night, they reveal that I had been sitting perfectly still, in a prolonged, vegetative state. For twenty-four hours, I had not moved from a chair.

27. PEPPERAMI

When I return home, I have to go to work but I am alternating between waves of anxiety, terror, panic and exhaustion. I am going through one panic attack after another, clutching my office desk like I'm trying to fly it through a snowstorm.

I'm sitting at my desk, on the verge of tears, when a giant sausage enters the room. It prances around the office. It seems to be talking to people, and people are talking back. I shout to no one in particular, 'Is everyone else seeing this?' It turns out that, yes, it indeed is a giant sausage. A snack company has sent their mascot (a giant, dancing 'Pepperami') to our offices to hand out free snacks for promotional purposes. The sausage approaches my desk, looks at me, and senses alarm.

'You all right, mate?' he asks.

'I don't know,' I tell him. I really don't know.

'Rough one, eh?' he says. ''Ave a pint. It'll calm ya down some.'

I take the sausage's advice, and race to the pub where I drain two pints immediately. I sit there and pray for all of this to end. And after a few days, it does.

Looking back on the trip, I know that for those three days of my life I probably cost myself a month of lifespan. This is a uniquely British way of living: you'll regret missing those three days, but you'll never remember that month. What's the point of living longer, if in fact you aren't really living it up?

And still, to this day, I don't feel right eating Pepperami, after all it did for me.

28. FAIRY CAKES

Elena and I have flown to New York, where we are due to be married at City Hall. There in line, along with other assorted immigrants, we wait in front of the clerk for our turn. We're supposed to be met by a handful of friends – a group of Americans and Brits. The Americans have shown up early. The Brits, Andy and his wife Caroline, are nowhere in sight. We are next in line, when I get a phone call from Andy.

'Can you hold off a bit? We're running late.'

I tell him we can't – if we get out of the queue, we lose our place, and the court is closing in thirty minutes.

'We're just moments away!' he yells.

But I say no. Brits are always late, and this time I can't afford to accommodate their tardiness.

How weird is that? I've never been in a hurry to commit to anything, and yet I can't wait to do this. Something has changed in me. I am pretty certain there is something about England that allowed me to fall in love, get married and settle down in a way that I wouldn't have been able to do in New York.

Back in Manhattan, the need to see what else is 'out there' always prevented me from seeing what I already had in front of me. Sounds like a pretty wordy fortune cookie, but it's true. Maybe England taught me to take notice when something wonderful happens, rather than wait until it's left me because I've become an ass. Which is how it normally works. Or perhaps it's the understanding that so much in life is crap, that you become really good at knowing when something is truly really good. Great, even. And Elena is great.

Thankfully, Andy and Caroline show up just as we get in front of the female judge, and in ten minutes the ceremony – a rote affair as romantic as a tax form – is over. We head to the best restaurant in town, then to a party at a club. There, Caroline presents us with a large cart of fairy cakes.

Fairy cakes are usually a sign of celebration, mainly at birthday parties for kids. Here in America, however, we don't call them fairy cakes – after all, if we did then no ten-year-old boy would touch them. We call them cup cakes, named I suppose because one is the same size as a 'cup'. This is what you call research, people. Learn from it.

These cakes have been altered a bit, though, for on top of each are two plastic figures, a bride and groom. Caroline and Andy have chosen two different sizes – the bride figurine is towering, and the groom dwarfish, to match Elena and myself. I should have never invited Brits.

29. THE CHRISTMAS CRACKER

Christmas approaches and the office is dead. Except for the drinking. That has escalated. Now, as a matter of course, instead of finding dried vomit on my doorstep, it's frozen solid. If you look real close at it (and I urge you to in order to experience the range of colours), frozen regurgitation looks like Superman's lair, with wonderful crystals and diamond-like shapes.

The hard part about drinking during the holidays is that every place is shut for private parties. Often I will walk by a local pub in the early evening, and peer in to see a group of sombre people sitting quietly as a man makes a speech. Hours later, however, these people will be urinating on car doors.

I didn't know the Brits had such holiday spirit, but I suppose any event that's an excuse to drink will be embraced by a Brit, even if the event tends to be dreadful. And I'm told Christmas parties are generally that.

Apparently the bad parts are obvious: the food is going to be bland and cold and the amount you pay will be more than you would have liked. You'll end up sitting next to someone you hate, and you won't ever find a cab home.

But Brits still look forward to Christmas parties anyway, perhaps because even though you are pessimists, you are also optimists about your pessimism. You actually look forward to seeing how bad things really are, and don't want to be disappointed by the awfulness of it.

Our dinner (which is, oddly, at lunchtime) is at an upscale burger joint. The tables are solid blocks of wood, and the chairs mildly uncomfortable – which is fitting because so are we. It is cold and cheerless, and as we take our seats we realize we are all far too sober.

There is an icebreaker on each place setting – something called a Christmas cracker. A shiny hollow thing made of cardboard and paper, it's a flimsy contraption that contains stuff. I have never seen one before. It looks delightful, and Jenni, a bubbly girl from a strange place called Wales, asks me to pull on the end of hers, and I do. After snapping it apart, I find a funny hat, a small toy and a joke within. Everyone's doing it. This is crap. But it's good crap.

After the meal, a numbers guy stands up and begins a speech about 'this year's figures'. It only takes one minute before he is hit by a chip. Thank God for booze, because booze encourages people to throw food, and throwing food is a perfect way to kill a speech. Toppings are now flying across the room, as the once placid group of employees turns dark and dangerous. Who knew pickles could do this to people?

After the bill gets paid by the boss, the crowd spills into the dissipating sunlight and fans out along the pavement towards a bar on Old Street. At this point I get a phone call from an American writer from a major New York paper. He's here on an assignment and wants to get drunk.

Once inside the bar, the drinks continue to pour, and out of pockets come the little packets of white powder. As trips to the toilet are made with increasing frequency, staffers return to dance wildly, gesticulating hands and swinging arms that soon turns into a form of wrestling. One guy, Lance, who lost the ability to speak moments earlier, tackles one of his underlings. They get separated, and something approximating words is exchanged. Meanwhile the American reporter jumps on to the dance floor, the victim of narcotic bravado. A dance contest between him and Lance ensues, until Lance careens out of control into a table of horrified women. Bouncers bundle him up and toss him on to the street. I look out the window, and he is shouting at trees. I sneak out to help him and am not allowed back in. It takes a forty-five-minute walk before I'm able to flag down a minicab. He's Jamaican, and he's listening to techno.

I think he's on something. The next day at work there are chocolates on every desk, courtesy of Lance. This is very British of him, I think. You attack your mates then you buy them chocolates. They are Cadbury's, the Christmas assortment. Lance has no memory of what he did last night but he did remember to buy chocolates. And that's the important thing.

30. THE BLACK CAB

I am taking a black cab across town to see my old friend Phil. When I call him to tell him I am on my way, the driver hears my accent and waits a few seconds before saying, 'What about your Mr Bush then?'

'Your Mr Bush.' It was as if I had actually built the man in my garage over the weekend. I know better than to defend Bush, even if he's no worse than any other politician on either side of the ocean. But Christ! How do cab drivers know so much, and care so much, about a guy from Texas who doesn't even live in your country? People in America think George Michael is your Prime Minister.

I am staring at the meter on the dashboard. It's clicking quickly, carving a deeper hole in my pocket. The black cab is a jaunty reminder to every visiting Yank that the American dollar is as weak as our beer. A ride across town, or even to Paddington Station from the flat on Wells Street, costs nine pounds, or around seventeen bucks. For seventeen bucks, I can fly to Prague on BMI, and still have enough cash left over to contract the human papilloma virus. This is why, despite hitting the cash-point every morning, by the evening I am wandering with empty pockets. My two big expenditures are the pub and the cab.

But I love the cabs. The interior exudes a cosy charm – a beautiful rejection of the repulsive filth we often refer to as Yellow Cabs in Manhattan. There is nothing more uncomfortable or wrong than a yellow cab. It is yellow to remind us, perhaps, that the driver probably peed himself. Black cabs never smell (other than of, perhaps, aftershave) but yellow cabs stink.

Black cabs defy logic. For one, they can turn in impossible places, at impossible angles. I don't understand how it's done but, if desired, a black cab can complete a full U-turn inside a countertop microwave. The ability of the cab to make absolute nonsense of logic and space almost makes the price paid worth it. Even though my address might be on the opposite side of the street, I always ask the cabbie to leave me on the nearest corner.

But they always refuse, because I think they enjoy doing U-turns in tight spaces.

During the ride the cabbie lectures me on George Bush. I don't respond, because I can't. It doesn't matter what the topic is – Israel, Iraq, mice – the blame can always be traced back to Bush. I agree with everything, despite not agreeing with most of it. His bald head bounces along, rising sharply every time he slows down and rolls over those jarring speed bumps marring the residential roads on the way to Muswell Hill. They make me nauseous, these 'sleeping policemen', as the driver calls them.

I'm thinking, I could bring up George Galloway or Ken Livingstone, both reprehensible nutbags. But why incite the man conducting me at 60 kph through streets laid out in the Jacobean age?

Now he's looking at me. He's actually turning around and talking, all while driving. He's no longer seeing the road.

If you're an American in the UK, you had better get used to this discourse, because you will attract Bush-haters like moths to a bug lamp. I never take it personally because, I'm thinking, it's all about rooting for the underdog. And when you love underdogs, you have to create overdogs. The US is the overdog, and it's the overdog the UK loves to hate.

The driver, inevitably, has moved on to the topic of immigrants. I nod my head a lot because now he is looking at me again. And laughing. I start laughing too – it's a complicit method of agreement. Then I abruptly tell him to 'toss me off' at the corner.

The driver pulls immediately to the left-hand side of the road, and looks down, silently. I look at the machine and the little red numbers read: £23. I step outside and give him £25.

Standing on the corner, I hand him the cash through the open passenger window, and off he goes. I love black cabs, if only for the fact that money exchanges hands on two feet. Nothing makes me feel more desperate than digging for coins in the back of a yellow cab as it pulls to the side of a busy road. In yellow cab world, we are expected to pay once the car pulls over and as quickly as possible. You get a much more civilized process with the black cab: the car stops, you get out, you pay – preventing the rush that inevitably leads to a loss of valuable belongings. Those formless back seats in yellow cabs seem to swallow everything from change to small children the moment you sink into them.

When an American yellow cab approaches, you never know how it's going to smell, what country the driver escaped from, and what strength of hash he's smoking. In England, the black cabs are so consistent in their lack of surprise, they're as comfortable as your living room sofa. When you get into one you may not be home yet, but you just as well might be.

The black cab driver may be a sociopath or worse, a racist, but for some reason I am convinced all of them are the smartest people in the British Empire.

'It's been that way since the Hackney Carriage licence system was set up some time back in the 1800s,' my British friend Chris explains.

I haven't done the research, obviously, but I'm fairly certain that a disproportionate number of winners on British quiz shows and radio phone-ins are London taxi drivers. I'm sure a quick survey of the contestants on *Who Wants to be a Millionaire?* would prove it.

Chris, like many of my new British friends, loves explaining 'the knowledge' – the rigorous, five-year course all drivers go on, in which they learn, by heart, every street name, permutation of route and shortcut in London.

'They have to pass a tough exam in the HQ in King's Cross in order to be admitted, and there's a higher burnout rate than the paratroopers or something,' Chris tells me.

This five-year fact-cram means they effectively train their brains to become insatiable fact-sponges, and they absorb almost everything they hear, or overhear, with brilliant powers of recall. This is also probably why they can't stop talking – they have to vent, like little knowledge volcanoes, to prevent themselves from hacking their families into tiny pieces. In America, the schooling New York cabbies get amounts to Koran lessons in a basement.

These drivers are not just chauffeurs – they're a whole dark, professional class to themselves.

'A guild of bastards,' is how Chris describes them. 'It's like you've got journalists as the fourth estate, and then cabbies, who are like the Masonic, black market anti-press in verbal form. They all share the same Victorian opinions, qualify every other noun with the word "fuckin", they hate everybody who isn't a licensed taxi driver and they all know, literally, everything. If they weren't so negative, cabbies would be ruling the country.'

A few days later I'm sitting at the pub and I see a colleague, Nick, limping towards me. I look down at his foot, which is gushing blood.

'I tried to jump a fence,' he explains, adding that on the other side was an errant spike.

Why did a twenty-five-year-old male decide to jump a fence on a Monday afternoon on a work day? He points to two blonde girls in short skirts. If you're going to impress women, I suppose, you should always try to jump something. The girls have left Nick now, and we flag down a black cab to get him to a hospital. And despite the sorry, drunken state of Nick, the cab pulls over and the window rolls down.

I am about to get in, but the driver waves me off.

'No worries, I'll get him there,' he says, and speeds off with a very drunk and bloody idiot inside.

31. THE DRUNKEN MAN

Elena wants me to take the bus and see the city. Without her to egg me on, I'd choose instead to simply sit at home and watch *Big Brother*, my new favourite show. But I would also probably not bathe, brush my teeth or eat anything other than Rustlers burgers. So now we're on the bus, and we're about to get off, or 'alight', in St John's Wood.

Stepping off and standing on a corner, I look up and down the street – one that is peppered with quaint shops. Everything around here, it seems, is quaint. Except for a man's voice, loud, throaty, yet inarticulate, coming at me from across the street. I look up and see a well-dressed man standing and staring at us, nodding as he screams at me. He is holding two shopping bags. I don't recognize him.

'Tosser!' he yells, so loud that shopkeepers come out to see the target of abuse. I now know what a tosser is, and I am pretty sure this guy thinks I'm one. I walk toward him.

'You OK?' I ask.

'Fuck off, tosser,' comes his reply.

'What's the problem?' I try once more.

'You're the fucking problem, mate! Fucking tosser!'

His eyes are bloodshot and watery, and he seems on the verge of laughing, but at the same time he appears genuinely angry with me. I don't get it.

Elena pulls my arm and says, 'Let's go, honey.'

A small crowd forms along the street and, being a guy, I feel I can't leave now.

'What . . . do you want to fight?' I ask.

'Fuck yes, tosser,' comes his quick response. I look at his hands. He is holding his grocery shopping. I can see tomatoes, a loaf of bread, and eggs.

'You can't fight holding your groceries.'

'Yes I fucking can, you tosser. Let's go!' he says, nodding.

His eyes are gently closing. A man in front of his shop stops sweeping, now genuinely interested.

'Let's go then,' I say. As I clench my fists, the man appears to have fallen asleep, standing, holding his groceries.

'I can't hit a man holding shopping bags,' I tell him.

'That's cos you're a fucking tosser,' he replies, eyes closed.

I look over at the people milling about and decide it's better to smile and leave.

As I turn and walk away, the man with the bags leaves me with, 'That's right! Go on, tosser!'

I look back a few times as we walk up the street, and there he is, still yelling. He may still be behind me right now, for all I know.

This is the first time I've been accosted by a drunken man in England, in the middle of the day. And it probably won't be the last. But it illustrates a key point: outdoor drunkenness may not be unique to the UK, but it's definitely far more entertaining. In the UK, drunks are far more selfless – they happily perform for you without asking. They are like the Royal Shakespeare Company, but with only slightly more projectile vomiting.

I can't make my mind up if I love UK drunks or hate them. I can say they make for an adventurous evening. Your drunks are 'unpredictable'. A smile can mean anything, from 'Have a seat' to 'I will kill you'. It's why when I walk into a pub for the first time I feel a little like the Dustin Hoffman character in *Straw Dogs*. I can read the danger in the air; I can feel it all around me. It's a slight buzz in my colon.

This brings me to a theory. In New York, people are assholes when they're sober, and become nice when they're drunk. In England, it's the opposite. People are nice when they're sober – soft-spoken, kind, helpful – but turn into monsters when they're drunk.

It's why every day and night the streets of London play out like a zombie flick. In the daytime everything's fine, and then right around 9 p.m. or so, when the pubs overflow, the glazed-eyed monsters rise up and roam the city, still dressed in their estate agent suits, puking and pissing up and down the street. On my road, I always find one sitting in the gutter with his head between his knees, his hair still spiky from that morning's bout with the styling gel. His mobile is still in his left hand, and he's trying to make a call to some girl he just met, while getting sick on his shoes. He's adorable.

So . . . I am surrounded by delightful young men who are mostly shy and dependable. Few raise their voices beyond a careful whisper. Pour three pints into them and that quiet reserve unravels. If I were a psychiatrist I would say that alcohol provides a conduit to allow repressed emotions to gush forth – and all the pent-up rage the Brits carry under a veneer of pleasantry breaks through. This explains my friend Jimi, who is in the pub as I write this, picking a fight with a sink.

Which reminds me of World War II. That was one of Britain's greatest achievements, and it was led by Winston Churchill, who was a major boozebag. Maybe the whole of the British army was blitzed while getting blitzed, which explains their immense bravery.

But I am not a psychiatrist. I mean, I'm not even bald or addicted to porn. In fact, I am a drunk. And as a drunk, I know that drinking in England has less to do with being drunk and more to do with getting drunk. Getting drunk is the Brits' only method of real communication – a chance to talk about their bands, their bosses, their favourite teams, without polite restraint. In America we drink to escape from our own intrusiveness. Conversely, the sober Brit gets drunk to approximate the intrusiveness of the sober Yank. This is the backbone of my other British drinking theory, that drunken obnoxiousness is inversely proportional to gentleness of character. The problems arise when, once you've gotten drunk, what do you do next?

32. VOMIT

I'm finally settling in to my neighbourhood. I'm getting used to
the loud Spanish couple having sex upstairs, so much so that I
don't really even notice it any more. I am learning to appreciate
the man who sings loudly outside my window every Friday at 11
a.m. He dresses like a court jester and strums a polka-dot guitar.
He sings about Iraq. It's amazing what George Galloway will do
for attention.

I appreciate the massage parlour I am pretty sure is operating
from the lower ground floor in the building across the street. The
girls go in and out, and they all speak Polish. Men sometimes
appear, walking out, looking satisfied. I have also grown fond of
the fat, half-naked man who every morning stares at me from the
second-floor window above the Japanese restaurant as I go and
get coffee. And, as I go and get coffee, I am even getting used to
the vomit I step gingerly over.

Vomit seems to be all around my neighbourhood. It comes in
all shapes and sizes, sometimes green, sometimes red, thick on
one day, thin the next. Each splat of vomit on my street, I realize,
is unique, just like a snowflake. A repulsive, slippery, chunky
snowflake.

The amount of street sleet normally increases from the middle
of the working week, starting roughly on Tuesday evening and
then culminating near the end, with Friday evening producing
the most splats per street. That means, usually, that Saturday is
always the worst day for your shoes. I wear two pairs and walk on
all fours.

This pattern of puke, which resembles a bell curve but with
lumps, can be attributed to the drinking that goes on after work,
which increases as the week progresses. I have noticed, at my
company, that when some men decide to swear off drinking for
the weekend (meaning Sunday, and possibly Monday), Tuesday
is when they 'get back on it'. There are only three days left in the
week, so why not celebrate? And they do. And I step around the
consequences the following morning.

During a typical summer week, it actually gets worse, peaking around Thursday. I try to count the number of splats, but I can't actually figure out if I am counting old vomit or new. Worse, restaurants usually hose down the streets, eliminating most of the evidence before I can make a proper tally. Plus there are stray dogs that know a free meal when they see one. This leads to another question: do dogs get drunk from eating human vomit? And, in turn, does that make them sick? Where, then, is the dog vomit? Do rats eat it? And does that make the rats puke?

Trick question: Rats are actually a non-vomiting species – they do regurgitate, though, which is sending undigested stomach contents back up to the oesophagus. I hear Anna Nicole Smith was really good at this.

The good news about all this vomit is that it provides me with my only form of exercise. Hopping to work on a Friday morning to avoid puked-up curry must qualify as an aerobic exercise, surely. Actually, I've looked it up and found out that hopping is a form of 'plyometric' exercise, like jumping or skipping. It burns more calories than walking. And it's more fun in a plaid skirt. This extra exercise means I can drink more, get sick, then spend the morning hopping around the sick, which burns calories, which then allows me to drink that much more in the evening. Circle of life, people. Circle of life.

33. SHIT TATTOOS

I'm meeting a man for a pint today. His name is Eoin McSorely, and he edits a magazine called *Front* – a ribald mix of tits and humour that burps out monthly and appeals to van drivers. Which makes sense, since Eoin, a strapping, bald, intimidating fellow, used to be a van driver himself. Judging from the amount of naked breasts in the mag, the van drivers probably steer with one hand.

I meet him at a pub because I want to hire him, mainly because he knows what 'lads' want more than I do: football, Page 3 girls, cheap pints . . . these are his top three desires too.

Eoin is one of those big and bald British guys who dislodges your kidney when he pats you on the back and always has a grin plastered across his face. Watching him drink pints is the equivalent of watching a hoover suck up dust. It's a smooth action, accomplished in a single movement. Of more interest, though, is they way he says 'bless' after every other sentence. This is all new to me.

'Did you hear about Johnny? Some cunt axed his face, bless.'

I cannot figure out if 'bless' is a sign of sympathy for the subject matter, or a mild jab. Originally it might have been religious, in the sense that one in strife or trouble should be blessed. However, the more I hear it from Eoin, I've come to realize its intention is condescending – affixing the word to finish sentences and punctuate your disdain.

'Did you hear about Johnny? He thought today was Saturday and didn't come into work. He got sacked, bless.'

I can now tell when Eoin finds people stupid or irritating – he always adds a 'bless' to their description: 'He means well, bless 'im.'

So you say the word because the person you are talking about needs help, but not of the biblical kind. Not any more, anyway. After all, Brits don't believe in God any more – you let Americans do that.

After our sixth pint, we are on to talking about tattoos and

Eoin tells me he has one. I look to his arms and hands but see nothing. He inserts his thumb into his mouth, pulls down his lower lip and flips it over, revealing 'Millwall' in primitive scrawl. I gather he always pulls down the lower lip after the sixth pint. Did it hurt? I ask.

'Probably, but you can reckon it was performed when I wasn't sober,' he says.

I've seen tattoos like this, usually among builders who are working in our offices, or rough-looking gentlemen in public houses. I recently met a scaffolder who had 'love' and 'hate' tattooed on his knuckles, and then tried to scrape them off with a knife. Now when he goes out in the sun any longer than ten minutes, the shadows of the letters swell up, and it's positively frightening.

If I were to get a tattoo, these would be the ones I'd get. The other, more professional kind – the barbed wire around the bicep or anything featuring Oriental lettering – are simply markers for morons. They're designed for people trying to appear rebellious, when in fact all they're doing is conforming to the current trends. I hate these people, and they do not frighten me. But people like Eoin who have shit tattoos, that's another story. Those tattoos require commitment, and a certain lack of scruples which, when combined, make a great person to have on your side during a brawl.

34. GINGERS

My favourite band at the moment is a hard rock outfit called the Wildhearts, and I desperately want to cover them in the magazine. The lead singer is an intense, charismatic gentleman who goes only by the moniker 'Ginger'. And yes. He has red hair.

I meet Ginger at – surprise – a dingy bar in London. We shake hands and I buy him a pint of Stella. He's a skinny fellow, around forty years old, decked out with tattoos and ropey red dreadlocks. We start drinking, and he fills me in on the last few years, which have taken their toll, as rock and roll does. I truly believe Ginger has written some of the best pop songs in the last twenty-five years.

He has a fiery disposition, which fits into the clichéd constellation of characterizations noted for all redheaded people, making them targets of derision from school kids to shopkeepers. Orangutans, squirrels and highland cattle are also redheaded, but no one makes fun of them.

In the US, we have no feelings, good or bad, about our redheaded brethren. We consider them nice people despite the fact their head resembles the working end of a plunger. But in the UK, there's a weird thing about redheads, or 'gingers' as you call them. I mean, what's with the way you pronounce the word? Why is the G pronounced hard, like 'Gutfeld', when it should be more like my mom's favourite drink, 'gin'?

One of my co-workers, Darren, has red hair, and every day he's reminded of it. He's around thirty. Shouldn't this have stopped when he was thirteen? It bothers you for ever.

'Even last night my ginger mate Chris suffered almost complete ostracization at a house party,' Dave tells me. 'It's not disdain, but the English just like to find any points of difference, no matter how insignificant, and blow them up to cartoon proportion.'

So, if you're a little bit overweight, then you're a massive fat bastard. If you are a girl and you have sex once, you're a big fat slag. If you're ginger-haired, your life is fucked.

I read that Prince Harry was bullied for being a ginger – and he's 'bloody' royalty. People have been stabbed for having red hair, and ginger families have had to move because of the abuse. I also read that the government doesn't bother with cases of discrimination against redheads, which strikes me as unfair. If anything, we should be directing our hatred toward albinos – who are far freakier to look at.

In contrast, you can't make fun of anyone in America without being fired, or slapped with a lawsuit. It's absolutely unfair that you Brits can still go around and target a minority group simply based on their atrocious hair colour, while we attend sensitivity seminars on how not to offend furniture.

So where did this all come from? During the Middle Ages, it is said red was the colour of the devil, and also a symbol of sexual perversion. Redheaded men are often painted as villains in fables, and red hair combined with green eyes meant you were a witch, or possibly a vampire. But the people I've talked to say the real reason behind the hatred for gingers comes down to two words: Mick Hucknall.

35. THE CORPSE

I try to make it to the gym – something I always did while I was in New York – but I never actually get there. I pack my gym bag and head out, but I almost always end up in the pub. It's actually impossible, I have found, to consider spending an hour or two on a stair climber after watching a large group of young people smiling and laughing in the street, standing in circles, staring at their shoes and holding their pints. The Brits don't take fitness seriously, but they do care about having fun. I can't think of a better thing to do right now in my life than standing outside the King and Queen, holding an ice-cold pint, talking about nothing in particular.

Yes, I said 'ice-cold' pint. I've noticed the pubs have introduced 'extra cold' lager into their pubs. It's not very British, which prides itself on lukewarm suds, but I wonder if these new chilled brews are designed to pacify foreigners like myself, who need everything cold.

Back in a previous life as editor of *Men's Health*, a fitness nut told me that for every minute you spend in the gym, you add a minute to your life. It always sounded like a pretty good deal, especially if your life at that point was a crashing bore. But living in London, I realize how bankrupt that idea is. The fact is, in London, life is good right now. And that minute you spend exercising is a minute you are taking from NOW and tacking it on to the part of life later one might call hell – those last few years when you're peeing into a clear plastic bag and mistaking your children for spiders.

The fact is, it's far better to be careful with your minutes while you're young and careless, when you're still able to pull drunken secretaries at the pub and sneak dope on to an aeroplane. The trade-off from 'now' to 'later' is wholly unnecessary and wrong; you won't want that extra time when it's spent straddling a steel bed pan, straining after every nugget of undigested bran. No. As the world moves on without you, you'll be praying for a quick death, one denied to you by your former self – the guy pumping relentlessly up and down on a stair climber. See, instead you should be pumping that admin assistant staggering out of the King and Queen with her skirt tucked into her underwear.

I have sacrificed the gym for the pub, and my biceps have withered while my liver has expanded. And the rest of my body is turning to mush. The suit I purchased at Gieves and Hawkes can no longer be buttoned up without excruciating pain. In it, I look like a tightly wrapped sausage. My body is appearing to go puffy and soft; the Yankee sinew sinking below the flab. I am turning British, acquiring the muscle tone of the leads in a Merchant Ivory film. The female leads.

So now, I think I am rejoining the gym. I started to get up early, a time when the pubs are closed, in order to resist temptation. But on my way to the gym in the morning, I notice something new. There are sick people in front of buildings and lurking around corners. They're holding on to IVs, some sitting in wheelchairs.

All of them are smoking.

Then, one morning, I spot a corpse being loaded into the back of a van. It isn't until I check my map that I realize my flat is located in between two large buildings labelled 'hospitals'.

It all makes sense now. All these sick people in my neighbourhood aren't there by choice. But what amazes me is that the sick refuse to stay in bed, and prefer the beauty of London streets, even if it means wearing pyjamas on Goodge Street. They're also smoking like chimneys. Sick chimneys, but chimneys nonetheless.

In America, sick people don't smoke. Healthy people don't smoke. In fact nobody smokes, because smoking is considered a far worse crime than genocide, racism and not recycling. I agree. Smoking is evil, made eviler by the fact that I can't stop doing it. But when I see these folks in their hospital gowns puffing away, suddenly I don't feel so hopelessly corrupt.

The hospital that belched out the corpse just closed, and they're turning the whole place into flats. I have no idea where they will put all those sick, smoking people. I suppose there's always Hull.

36. OLD PEOPLE

When I was younger, I had no idea where old people came from. I didn't think old people were just folks who had been around longer than me. I thought old people were old from day one, and just remained old until they died. I also assumed that I would always be young; that I would look the same from the day I knew I was a person to the day I would cease existing. Being old was for old people. Not for me. I would be young for as long as I knew myself as me. Imagine my shock when I hit twenty-five and they told me the truth!

I held this belief because, aside from a set of parents, I never saw people who occupied the space between 'young' and 'old'. Also: 'old' people were never allowed out. So I looked at them much in the way most people look at parrots.

But now I am changing my mind. In Britain I see old people everywhere, and this has forced me to adjust my system of beliefs towards ageing, a system that protected me from assuming I age at all. Now, however, at the age of forty-something, living here in England, I have gotten dramatically fatter, balder and wrinklier. I am turning into a fig. I now think that the moment you admit you're getting old, you suddenly are old. And prune-like.

This can't be a bad thing, getting old. Being young is too demanding. In order to be young, you have to look young, and that's expensive and time-consuming. It is much better to give up, give in, and let yourself go. In this way, I have become British. England is an old man, one that stopped caring about the crap you care about when you're young.

Except when it comes to attire. In England many old men still dress like old men, in suits and ties. In America, more old farts are dressing like their grandsons – baseball caps and shorts from Urban Outfitters. A neat comparison: Charlie Watts and Jack Nicholson. One dresses like a country gentleman, the other like a fat German twelve-year-old at a weight-loss camp.

Even British kids sound far older than they should. This is because English accents sound like something that comes with age (much like varicose veins and affection for commemorative plates). It's a funny thing that most Yanks think British kids are really, really smart because they have accents like Alistair Cooke, Julia Child and other people who lulled us to sleep on public broadcasting when we were little. I am intimidated by British children, especially when they travel in packs. They sound erudite, even while beating me up and taking my mobile.

But if I am going to become older (it's happening as I write this) I might as well do it here, in England. Because only in Britain can you be old and get away with it. In America, old people are not allowed outside air-conditioned spaces. We corral them into armed pens like Arizona or Florida or wherever it's hot and they can complain about the heat. In the US it's pretty much a crime to be old. Or at least, look old.

It's different here, or at least on my street. There's one elderly man who walks laps around my building. He's up every morning, dresses impeccably, and uses a cane, as he hits the pubs around Fitzrovia. He used to run a big club in Piccadilly and has a lot of stories, like old people should.

'Frank Sinatra was always a generous man. Every week when he played, he tipped us £200,' he tells me at a table in the King's Arms one wasted afternoon. 'But Yul Brynner, what an asshole.'

I see him every day and we talk but, for some reason, he still doesn't say hello to me when we cross paths. He doesn't acknowledge my existence. I admire that.

I also admire the fact that old people don't leave the city simply because they're outnumbered by the young. I admire the fact that old people get up earlier than I do, put on suits and go to the park and read, when they should be dead. I like the idea that incontinence does not prevent them from drinking, a lifestyle choice I am getting down pat.

Nothing makes me happier than seeing an old person on the street, and running over to them, patting them on the head and feeding them nuts and old pieces of bread. I love seeing them in pubs. In the US, you don't run into old people at bars. Old people go to old people places. Young people go to young people places. In the UK, any pub is full of a comfortable mix of ages, from the loudmouth salesman to a seasoned crone with a diseased dog.

Which always makes for a fun evening. Right now, at the King and Queen, an elderly magistrate is taking a liking to my friend Dave. I am watching the short rotund old man with scraggly white hair moving in close for a kiss. He drags his hand along Dave's cheek and pleads for one. Dave is drunk, but not that drunk. He pulls back, and the old man looks sad.

'You're a fucking judge,' Dave says to the old man, who is trying to pull Dave into a corner. I watch, from a table filled with co-workers. The judge realizes he's being watched by six laughing men, and runs out of the bar, looking slightly ashamed. Dave retreats into the bathroom and gets sick.

This would never happen in the States, I tell my friends. For one, the judge is too old to be in a bar with young men. Or, if he was, he would at least have trimmed his eyebrows.

37. THE TV TAX LICENCE

I just saw a flaccid penis, and it wasn't mine. It's OK. Flaccid penises are totally legal on prime-time television. It's true – according to some rule, it's perfectly OK to show male frontal nudity unless the member is erect. I don't understand this rule, since flaccid penises are far scarier-looking than erect ones. At least when they're erect, their intentions are loud and clear. You can't trust a flaccid penis. Neville Chamberlain proved that.

'I have very prominent nipples, so losing one was like losing a finger.'

A lady in her sixties called Linda is saying this, right now, on the telly. I am watching *The Trouble With My Breasts*. While she is talking she is serving fish and chips to her husband. She is doing this topless. Her breasts, saggy and tattooed, seem perfectly happy on TV. She tells us that she is a nudist who needs to express herself without, she adds, upsetting children.

And so she moved to France.

British television rules the universe. Every day I find something new and exciting to watch – and so I find myself watching more and more television, and working less and less.

I even like Ceefax. I found it by accident, by hitting a button when I meant to hit something else. What a neat little world it is, like a telegram from a lost planet, it features a few static pages of text-based info on weather, finance and horse racing. It's the internet for television. Or rather, the phone book for people without phones. Or maybe it's a cookbook for people without ovens. I'm not sure any more, but it's still entertaining.

I've just finished watching *Big Brother*, and now I'm currently watching a prime-time programme devoted to the making of Queen's album *A Night at the Opera*.

The show is fantastic. Brits could do a show about anything and make it riveting. Even *Columbo* seems better over here, which makes no sense at all since it's, you know, American. So, I suppose, that makes me an idiot.

I got a letter today, something about a television tax licence fee.

Apparently once I bought a television, the government was notified. Talk about Big Brother, for real.

So I called the number on the bill to find out what I'm being taxed for. According to the gentleman who picked up, he told me that it's a tax levied by the government to help pay for programmes that don't get any funding from commercials. Essentially, we are talking about shitty programmes. In England, the TV licence was originally called a radio licence. Thankfully, I don't own a radio, or that would be taxed too.

I wrote a cheque for about £130, which is a little over two hundred bucks. It would have been cheaper if I had owned a black and white television, but who still owns one of those, aside from blind people? On that note, I read that blind people only have to pay half the fee, since they only use half their available senses.

According to my sloppy research, you can get arrested if you don't pay the tax. And I read somewhere that this actually happens – something like a few hundred people a year 'get nicked' for not paying. I would hate to get arrested for watching *Emmerdale* without paying. Nothing impresses an incarcerated crack dealer from the back alleys of Kingston more.

But as much as I hate taxes, I will pay. Because I have no choice. And British television is the best in the world. I love everything, including the junk. I love the junk even more, simply because the English accents fool me into thinking I'm watching something educational. In Great Britain, a common builder sounds more articulate than an American professor. But that's largely because American academics are lunatics.

I spend most of my time obsessing over my favourite show, *Big Brother*. We have the same show in America, but it rots. So here, in Britain, I never gave it a second thought, until my boss's wife implored me to watch it. Now I'm a blithering, pathetic fan.

There is something uniquely British about *Big Brother*. It's like London, an appealing set resembling a posh hotel, yet filled with the lowest of the low: pop star pervs, park bench fiddlers and frantic finger-sniffers. It's like they went to Regent's Park at midnight and emptied the bushes into a van.

I realize that many people find the show reprehensible, what with it glorifying in the weakness and bigotry of others, but so what? I am a hopeless fool infatuated with a programme that caters to the need for ridiculing anyone who has a dream of becoming famous.

We all want to be famous, I think, and because we aren't, we feel the need to take it out on those who try. Ever more fascinating are 'celebrity housemates', who exemplify the new British entertainer: grotesque but often likeable failures, willing to do almost anything to get their name in print.

The latest trend seems to be towards masturbation, for I have seen it three times on *Big Brother* alone, and once in a documentary that occurred during a network's 'Wank Week'. (In that show, a man fruitlessly attempted to pleasure himself, defeated only by his micro-sized member. I think the show was called *Me And My Small Penis*.)

Big Brother is wildly successful, especially among my friends – we talk about it non-stop at work and down at the pub. Elena and I Sky Plus every single moment, in case we miss anything. We also vote to evict housemates each week (at roughly fifty pence a pop). Sometimes Elena will vote more than once, depending on how much she hates a person, or how many we've been drinking.

We also adore *Big Brother's Big Mouth*. Russell Brand is the most interesting person on the planet, if only because I believe there are things living in his hair. I am sad that he no longer does the show, but at least I don't have to hear my wife tell me how good-looking he is.

The US version of *Big Brother* is no comparison. It even employs a music soundtrack, a dramatic method of alerting the viewer that something ominous is approaching. The UK version does not require such props. Why would you, when you're a fat blonde who, after guzzling wine, strolled out to the front lawn and sodomized herself with the empty bottle? A thoughtful girl – she still recycled.

Big Brother is interesting because Brits are interesting. You seem to have an endless supply of troubled family entertainers with sordid pasts, pop singers suffering from gender confliction and bad collagen implants, as well as whacked-out lefty politicians like George Galloway, who for one brief moment pretended to be a cat. It was a great moment for television, politics and people who hate George Galloway, which is anyone with an IQ higher than their age.

And then there's the bitchy girl who just got evicted – whatsherface. She lives around the corner from me on Great Titchfield Street. She has a terrific body, but a face that could scare the fur off a cat. I often heckle her when she walks by. What in God's name is wrong with me?

I, like everyone else, want to be around someone who's been 'on telly'. I'm not sure if it has anything to do with the fame they've acquired, or the novelty that previously we've only dealt with them as tiny characters on a flat screen, and now we're seeing them in all their 3D, average-height glory. I get excited whenever I see a British celebrity, no matter how insignificant. In fact, the lower they are on the totem pole, the more I like them. Oh look, there's Toby Young on Goodge Street!

Not everyone watches *Big Brother*, however. I do run into a few pseudo-intellectuals here and there who make a point of telling you they never watch it, as if they've been spending all that saved time in Africa digging irrigation ditches. But I don't watch *BB* to make myself feel smarter. I watch it because it's an amazing sociology lesson about modern Britain. Each contestant represents an English type – even the gay Canadian ones.

But I've also learned something about me, and my time spent so far in London. My hours are spent doing a lot of watching. I'm watching television. I'm sitting at the pub, watching people. I spend the mornings reading the paper. I am a comfortable spectator, watching life pass, without much interest in participation.

Over in America, I know the game is still playing, but for me, I'm more inclined to observe.

Enough navel-gazing. The good news is, the next *Big Brother* is just weeks away. I predict the cast will include someone who might have slept with Calum Best and a large clam. I put my money on the clam.

38. CLOUDS AND TRAMPS

The UK has four seasons. I've been here for around five and I can say that I have had approximately 15,450 conversations about the weather, usually in the elevator or in places that resemble the size and depth of an elevator (any flat). I'm looking out the window and watching the rain start and then stop. And then start again. Rain in the UK is like sun in the US. Except wetter.

Because the UK weather changes every seven minutes, it allows for endless conversations, all somehow related to the weather. My theory is that in the UK everyone talks about the weather in order to avoid talking about themselves. In the US everyone talks about themselves to prevent talking about the weather. Personally I'd rather hear how bad it looks outside instead of how bad you feel inside.

But after a few months of talk about clouds, I realize you could probably talk about clouds until you die. But, I just don't get the moaning. The weather here is pretty great. It's never as cold as it is in New York. It's also never as hot. There's no humidity, which in New York helps to create a phenomenon called wee-steam – an insidious vapour-like cloud that rises from the sewers to assault your nostrils with the stench of urine. In the middle of August, around 40th and 8th Streets, you can pretty much slice off a piece and eat it.

Right now, I'm on a trip to New York, looking into a TV gig that may or may not happen. It's hotter and stickier than a freshly soiled diaper. The sun bakes the cement on 8th Avenue and sends heat up your legs and along your chest as sweat drips down. In minutes I've already soaked my underpants. I'm here for some interviews, and I wish I could be back in London, watching instead of doing.

In the UK, even though the weather is never that harsh, the moaning about it never stops. Yes, the purpose of British weather is to allow people to moan about British weather. The British, as a rule, hate whiners or 'whingers', so all that unsatisfied energy has to be focused somewhere. And that somewhere is up there.

A word of warning, however: looking up at London's low, dirty, but somehow beautiful clouds can be dangerous (at least in my neighbourhood). I am referring to two things:

1. Traffic: which innately senses foreigners. I am amazed how most cars go out of their way to steer around smartly dressed British men and women on their way to work, only to come veering after me. Today, my first day back from the States, I stupidly revert to my old 'look right instead of left' manner of crossing the street. It's a wonder I'm not strapped to a chair writing this book with a pencil glued to my forehead.

2. Tramp faeces: which I tend to step in whenever I'm wearing new shoes and find myself staring up at the sky thinking about clouds. Hopping across the street, I land in a pile, and smear it across the bottom of my shoe. I inspect the damage, and realize that no dog could have left this.

In the US, the word 'tramp' no longer exists. We instead favour the word 'homeless', because we think everyone should have a home, if only to park their shopping cart. The UK tramps, however, make no claims for victimhood. They seem to enjoy it, like our hobos of old. Their use of please and thank you is impressive. It might be a good idea to send America's rude children to live with UK tramps, if only to learn correct grammar and manners. Having spent time in both countries, I can compare the homeless from each place.

While UK tramps are eccentric, US homeless are homicidal maniacs. Yours are essentially harmless. Ours are faeces-flinging psychopaths. In front of Port Authority in midtown Manhattan last week a man layered in filth attempted to dance with me. He looked a little like he sprouted from a sewer drain. He was also fondling himself. In London, on my street, I am graced by a homeless crazy person whose only sin is singing, which he does loudly every Friday at 11 a.m. He's as good as anything on *X-Factor*.

It seems that in London the disdain for competitiveness even trickles down to the tramps. The act of striving against others for the purpose of achieving success, however, is still alive and well on the streets of Manhattan. That's the curious thing about the American homeless – despite not having a home, they are intensely materialistic. Even among the destitute you find go-getters: street people with more belongings than me. In New York, my local transient parks his shopping cart near me, and it's full of pots, pans, cushions, suitcases, canes, crutches and oil cans. More enterprising homeless have graduated from the cart to the wheelie bin, usually with a pallet strapped underneath to carry more goods.

I can only conclude that the London tramp is far less material-istic and competitive than his Manhattan counterpart, which has to be a good thing, I think, for their mental state. The British homeless seem happy with their lot, even if there isn't much of it. The most I ever see a 'tramp' holding in London is a few copies of the *Big Issue* and his pants.

39. IRN-BRU

Back at the office – it's Monday – I'm looking at a bottle of Irn-Bru that's sitting on one of my employees' desks. It is an alarming fluorescent orange shade, the same colour as Jordan and Jodie Marsh in wintertime. My copy chief, Chris, drinks a bottle of it a day and, when I ask him why, he has no explanation. I'm not even sure he believes it tastes that good. I take a swig and it's not half bad. I expected it to taste like a liquefied substance used in children's chemistry sets. It doesn't. Although it is only slightly better.

Apparently this beverage is Scotland's biggest-selling soft drink (there's even an ice-cream flavour), loved by Russians, and drunk by Brits to alleviate hangovers, which for them occur almost hourly. According to historians, the formula for Irn-Bru is a closely guarded secret, but its ingredients include 0.002 per cent of ammonium ferric citrate (a compound used for water purification and printing), caffeine, sugar, flavouring agents and colouring. The colouring could be anything, but I'm assuming it's derived from ground-up goldfish.

Kerin informs me that the Scots drink Irn-Bru to appear 'posh'.

'Having a beverage that is bright orange means you're rich,' he tells me.

Sometimes I think Kerin tells me these things to see how stupid I am.

But my fascination with Irn-Bru has a purpose: for it reveals yet another facet of British devil-may-care attitude that deviates from us Yanks. I doubt whether you could sell Irn-Bru in the States. It would probably be made illegal, if regulators ever got around to figuring out what the hell it actually was. I wanted to know about this concoction, so I did what any seasoned researcher would do: I hopped on the internet and went to wikipedia – a stunningly reliable research tool run by pale, anonymous shut-ins who still live at home with their parents. According to Wikipedia, although some US companies import the beverage, the Food and Drug Administration lists the stuff as a banned substance because it contains Ponceau

4R. Ponceau 4R is also banned in Norway. Norway, by the way, prides itself on its fermented trout.

Then again, I'm thinking: if something is seemingly bad for you, at the very least let us decide whether we want it or not. The US bans everything to a point now where, if you plan on wearing a helmet, you better be wearing a helmet under that helmet. And don't forget the seat belts and the knee pads. You'll need to wear those when purchasing more seat belts and knee pads. In the US, the obsession with living longer has pretty much created a nanny state. In England, however, everyone smokes, drinks and fights. It's like an old pirate movie, but without the scurvy. Somehow, Irn-Bru fits into this whole lifestyle. It's a scary-looking drink with a demented name (I was told it was once called Iron Brew – but they had to change the name because it didn't contain any iron). I imagine it's the perfect thing to drink after accidentally ingesting a wasp. To kill the wasp, of course.

'I drink it because I am half Scottish,' Chris says. 'Barr, the Glasgow fizzy drinks factory that makes Irn-Bru, is the wellspring of Scottish national pride!' Also, he says drinking Irn-Bru is thought to make you superhumanly hard. 'This is partly to do with the taste, but also thanks to an eighties advertising campaign whose slogan, delivered in broad Glasgow-docker, was: "Barr's Irn-Bru: made in Scotland, from girders".' Buried deep in the British national consciousness is the idea that a man who drinks Irn-Bru is a man who can drink rust.

The name is also confusing and unpronounceable to 'Sassenach scum', which is how Chris describes the English.

40. THE MOBILE DISCO DJ

I'm at a house party somewhere in South London, where they've got a young skinny white man spinning records. A few young girls surround him, and he's got one hand on his headphones, pressed up against his ears, looking very intense. The next song he's playing may be the most important song in the world. I hope it's not 'Glass Tiger'.

I'm with a few friends from work, and I'm sitting on the sofa, watching this kid spin records.

'Does he live here?' I ask Kevin.

'No,' he tells me. 'He's just the DJ.'

Do people actually hire other people to spin records at small house parties? In America, at 'keggers', we usually just appoint someone at the party to be in charge of the music. When he's too drunk to continue, we throw him out into the yard and appoint someone else.

'In the UK we don't ever want to run the music at parties,' Kevin says. 'Someone will always threaten you or physically remove your music for their own. You pay a DJ to play the music for you. This way he takes the shit away from you.'

DJs exist solely to get the grief. But they also exist to play music everyone likes – instead of just a few plums who only wish to play 'microhouse' or 'Kwaito freestyle'.

This is another area of UK life that confounds me: the elaborate splintering of music into tiny sub-genres that actually, for some reason, make sense being splintered. There's dark house, deep house, dream house, UK hard house and something called Nu-NRG. Don't forget progressive trance, ambient house and minimal techno. What about hard dance, hardcore, industrial, breakbeat and clownstep? There are about one hundred other sub-categories – it's like splitting hairs, except the hairs make noise.

Since I've been in England, I've met quite of few of these DJs – often via the young women they're dating (meaning, they're living with them and not paying rent) – and more than likely they're 'skint' and have to get by selling drugs. They are invariably skinny and covered in spots. They always have a record bag with them, looking like something Domino's uses to deliver pizzas, and they treat their records like the soft spot of a baby's head. If Kevin is right, and becoming a mobile DJ makes you the target of abuse, then by the looks of it, they probably deserve it. But I do admit they perform an admirable service. I'm going to hire one to play at my house, and throw knives at him.

41. THE QUEUE

It's a clear sunny Sunday afternoon, and I'm taking Elena to London Zoo. When we get there, we find a queue that stretches out past the zoo entrance and halfway down the road. Before I proceed, I would like to point out that I am using the word 'queue' instead of 'line'. I am doing it out of courtesy, even though having to type 'queue' takes at least twice as long as 'line' because it's full of repetitive vowels that force you to bounce back and forth on the keyboard. This proves how much I love England and vowels.

This particular queue is one that takes the wind out of you. It doesn't seem to be moving, and it's four or five people across. If I were alone, I would have given up and headed to the pub. But Elena is with me, and if there's a universal rule it's that a man would never queue for anything unless there was a woman forcing him to do it.

Women don't mind standing in queues. To them it's just an opportunity to check out other women's shoes and apply make-up. But for men, it's torture. We can't even check out the women, because we would risk death, as we are already with a woman. For me, non-moving queues create the worst kind of hopelessness. If hell exists, you can bet it is a queue.

So here we are, at the end of the queue, behind an armada of baby strollers and Muslims in full burkhas. The heat is stifling, but they seem completely relaxed, under a pile of black layers. I think they have portable fans underneath.

As we stand for half an hour, no one seems to complain. I try my best to relax, and I do this by biting my nails until they bleed. As we turn a corner, the queue splits into four parts (each one going to its own individual payment counter). Of the four new queues, the queue we choose turns out to be the only one not moving nearly as quickly as the others. The other lines stream by full of happy, chatty families. Some of these people arrived twenty or even thirty minutes after we did, and our line transforms into a stymied block of bitterness.

Forty minutes pass, and we have not moved. I am sweating, and now smoking, and I can tell from the look on Elena's face that she regrets marrying me. I am falling apart. There is some hold-up at the front of the line – it looks like someone tried to pay with a credit card, but the machine couldn't read it, and now they have to call in a technician. At this point, I think it's time to make a move.

I detach from our line and blend into the fast-moving one on the left. It all seems to work, even with the dramatic sighs and throat-clearings it causes from the rear. So far, no one is calling me on my queue jumping. Until, inevitably, I hear 'Excuse me! Excuse me!' in a distinct accent that could only belong to an American woman. She will not let up. I try to appear deaf, but now she's getting louder, and the glares are burning holes into the back of my scalp. It's time to give in. I turn around and meet the countless pairs of glaring eyes. They win, I lose.

After a good hour or so, we finally make it to the counter and pay for the right to stare at monkeys that will never, ever, have to stand in a queue for anything. They seem to mock me from behind their protective fences. I'm still pissed about being yelled at, yet part of me admires Americans for speaking up. But this incessant need to get involved has a downside. And that downside is being yelled at for queue jumping.

Thing is, a queue only becomes a queue if there's another person wanting the same thing you do. The key, then, is to develop hobbies, interests and dietary habits that are repellent to everyone else. Morris Dancing, for example. There's never a queue for that. And for good reason. Morris Dancing is a strange form of rhythmic stepping often accompanied by sticks and/or tobacco pipes with bells on. I saw it once, and I was scarred for life.

So if that's not appealing, and you cannot be in a queue alone, at the very least enjoy the fact that the misery you experience will be shared by someone else. Living in London, I have developed a few favourite queues. Right now I am at an HSBC bank, and the line is moving fast. This bank line has a delightful maze configuration – a queue that conjures up memories of my summer visits to Disneyland. These were the queues we spent hours in to get on to the Matterhorn or Pirates of the Caribbean. I still get a rush of excitement when I join that bank queue, even if all I get is a receipt for a deposit, instead of a 100-metre straight drop into a lagoon. This kind of queue works because it keeps people from spilling on to the street – a common problem with a single-file queue – and it allows you to stare at the people on the other side of the velvet ropes, shooting them a glare of superiority that says: 'I'm well ahead of you, and will be quickly out of here and on to better parts of my life while you're still here, waiting.' It's a satisfying feeling, one that you cannot indulge in when you're in a single-file queue.

I am now at the bank of windows, and I am greeted by the teller, who is looking at my deposit slip as though she has never seen one before in her life. For some reason, British bank tellers always make you feel like it's their first day at work – a hint that you will never see that deposit ever again. I do believe they are good at their job; they just prefer you to think otherwise. That lightens the workload for everyone.

I am now waiting for the bus. I hate bus queues because they always dissolve into chaos once the transportation arrives. These queues are seemingly orderly but, once the bus is in view, they turn into survival of the fittest meets *Lord of the Flies*, since those who are best at getting to the front of the queue tend to be feisty, dangerous children. Children in groups scare me. The total is greater than the sum of its parts. Throw five kids together, and you've got Mothra.

I need a drink. The queue for a drink can be the worst kind of queue, because it really isn't a queue at all, but a belly-up-to-the-bar process relying solely on the wits of the bartender to discern who is next. At pubs like the King's Arms and the King and Queen this is no problem. The bartenders are pros at seeing who deserves to be served first. At gastropubs, however, it's the opposite. Not only do you have innocents working behind the bar, you also have snooty customers paying for one half pint with a debit card – two factors that can turn any afternoon potential for drinking into hellish sobriety.

Right now I am at the Crown and Sceptre on Foley Street and it's about 6 p.m. I have been standing for ten minutes waiting to be served, and the bartenders continue to look beyond me, perhaps because I am short. Behind me, a man fresh from his job at the hip media company around the corner is reaching over and putting a glass of wine on his debit card. I want to beat him to death with a roast veal chop with cardamom pilaff and mushroom cream sauce. That's on the menu, and it's overpriced.

I am home now and on the phone, waiting in another queue. I enjoy waiting on the telephone because, unlike American counterparts, the automated operator has a British accent and lets you know exactly where you are.

'Your call will be answered in under one minute,' says the voice of efficiency, which is moderately erotic. It doesn't, however, make up for the real live Scottish person you end up speaking to, who is impossible to understand. For a Yank, it's like having a conversation with a word-mangler – the linguistic equivalent of a juicer.

Have you ever experienced queue panic? That's when there are two queues coming from separate directions to form one queue. (This happens, briefly when you enter and exit an aeroplane, for example.) Who ends up first in the queue when both queues converge? Even when you know you're in the right queue, you feel that the people in the other queue feel the same way (they are wrong). These things eat me up.

In the end, queuing has taught me how to be a better person. I am learning not to care too much about when you're supposed to be somewhere – not normal thinking for me. I need to be first. I often arrive to events hours early, just to make sure I'm the first in. I can't stand the idea of people getting anywhere before me. I used to fake being sick to board an aircraft early. It works every time. But queues in England beat that problem out of me. I no longer need to be first, because now I know it's not possible. No matter how early I arrive for an event, someone is always there before me. Standing in a queue is the equivalent of going to the gym, but instead of building your biceps you're pumping up your patience. Just tell yourself that, over and over again.

42. BENYLIN

When you get up in the morning and you stare at your jeans on the floor, and then you look at your sweatpants on the chair, and you choose to put on your sweatpants, then you are officially a fat person. Wearing sweatpants is an avoidance of belt notches, and belt notches are the real barometer of how truly fat you have become.

So, right now I am wearing sweatpants to the supermarket. And when you wear them in July, things are bad. Full-length mirrors in the bedroom only make it worse; I can see my ass, which resembles the face of Ukrainian opposition leader Viktor Yushchenko, after the poisoning. I cover it immediately to keep it from shocking Elena.

I used to be so fit. But that was a year and a half ago, and the accumulation of beer, bread and chips has turned me into little more than connective tissue stretched over a pub bin. I have become, I think again, British, at least in personal habits. Which is why I am at the chemist. That's where you go when you're British and you'd rather not go to the doctor.

Which is how the British deal with doctors: by avoiding them, because it's nearly impossible to see a good one without paying through the armpit. So you go to the chemist, who seems to have an answer for everything, no matter if the answer turns out wrong.

In America, a chemist is called a pharmacist. But these days, at least, real pharmacists are few, having been replaced by clerks who don't know the difference between lymphopathia venereal and tropical bubo (this is a trick question: there is no difference, as I can personally attest). Chemists in the UK seem not only smarter than our pharmacists, but more competent than doctors in general. At least, that's the impression I get at Shiva Pharmacy. The man behind the counter is a friendly Asian man, calm and knowledgeable. If he told me incontinence was cured by eating a pillow, I would believe him. Perhaps this is an illusion only bought into by Yanks, due to the name 'chemist', which in America actually means someone trained in chemistry. The closest most Americans get to chemists is their chemistry teacher – usually an old man who only retires after he's blown off his remaining hand.

I am at the chemist because my ears are clogged with wax, and maybe an insect or two. He points me to the 'candling', waxy funnels sitting on the counter. It costs six pounds for two of these 'candles', one for each ear. The pharmacist tells me that I should lie on my side, insert the funnel into my ear, and set the funnel on fire. The burning funnel somehow creates a vacuum that sucks the wax out of the ear.

I take the funnels home, and do as the man says. As the funnel burns, I hear a pleasant crackling and bubbling . . . it must be working! After a few minutes, I turn over and do the other ear.

It doesn't work. My ears are still plugged. In fact, I think I've made it worse. I call a real doctor and he tells me 'those things are worthless', and instructs me to come in. I sit down, and he pulls out a mechanical device like a dental drill, and jams it into my ear. Within minutes I can hear again.

There is a lesson here, I think. The more pleasant your chemist, the more likely you'll buy something that doesn't work. This is why, I think, you need to re-evaluate your unpleasant doctors. The more aloof your doctor is, the more likely he'll rid you of your sickness. But what do I know? I really only go to the chemist for a few things, one of which is Benylin.

People groan about the state of health care in the UK, and for the most part they're right. Universal health care is a joke, because if you really need something bad, you've got to wait for ever for it. You may have to pay through the nose for health care in the US, but at least you won't lose your nose in the process.

But what doesn't suck is Benylin. I bought it today to tackle a cough, and now I'm flying. I love this stuff. Instead of going out, I may simply drink straight from this bottle and hallucinate. It not only gets rid of your cough, but everything associated with a cough, along with short-term memory, speech control, the ability to walk and understand road signs. There's nothing in America that comes close, unless you count heroin. And we know that's too big a commitment. The only downside to Benylin is the hangover. My head hurts a lot. It only goes away, though, if I take more Benylin. I just have one question: why are the walls melting?

43. PORK SCRATCHINGS

My descent into the soft, puffy and bloated life continues. I have grown a pair of breasts that could qualify me for Page 3. I stare at myself in the bathroom mirror, and blame my increasing obesity on a number of things but mostly on two: my inactivity and bacon. In America, we have only one kind of bacon. In the UK, there are over 200 kinds: the most commonly ordered being streaky, smoked, green, dried and cured. I love it. Variety is the spice of life. All that bacon to choose from . . . it's almost impossible to get sick of it.

Pork has become a big part of my life, and so it's no surprise I'm turning into a porker myself. You are what you eat, say health gurus, and if that's the case, then I am only weeks away from becoming a Gloucestershire Old Spot, a large spotted pig native to England well known for its milk production and succulent arse.

I am turning into beer-soaked bacon, cured by cigarette smoke – the only flavour of pork I've yet to see in the UK. Is this how all flavours are invented? My meat is probably tender and flavourful due to the fact that when I am fat, drunk and sitting in a pub I'll eat almost anything. It has taken me well over a year and a half of sitting in the King and Queen to get over my fear, but I finally try pork scratchings. Being a pig myself, it qualifies as cannibalism.

'Here, try them,' says my mate, Eoin, throwing a bag at me, purchased at the King and Queen bar.

I am drunk, so I'm pretty sure I can do this. I read the bag, and inspect its contents. A pork scratching, as you probably already know, is a deep-fried pork rind that's eaten cold. In the US we sell big bags of things called pork rinds, which are puffy and light – the exact opposite of the UK pork scratching, which is dense and crispy. I suppose there is a metaphor in all of this – the culinary approach to this vile pork product reflects the different way our countries deal with everything. In the US, everything is over-sized and soft; in the UK everything is small and hard. I am not sure if this holds true with all things, but it certainly rings true with snack foods, bars and football fans.

I don't like American pork rinds, but I am going to give these scratchings a chance. I bite into one and chew, and feel its salty dampness pollute my mouth. I don't think I've previously experienced something so inedible on my tongue. I push it down with beer. And start again. Another awful bite, but this one feels a little fuzzy. I look into the bag, and I see tiny pricklings of hair pointing out of the snacks. I am not joking – there are hairs in my bag, on something I'm supposed to eat.

I still continue to eat them, although my face is set in a constant grimace.

'Aren't they awful?' says Eoin, as he shoves more into the hole in the front part of his large bald head. This is English life in a nutshell, or rather, a crinkly bag. The scratchings, like the weather and football, provide an avenue for moaning that works purely as a therapeutic tool. Eating these snacks allows you to take part in something horrible just so you can moan about how horrible it is. You take pleasure in moaning about something without hurting anyone's feelings or boring them to tears with your problems. Without pork scratchings, what would you talk about? Your job? Your wife? Your bills? That would just make you an American – the type of person who goes to a therapist to moan about stuff that's actually good. Here, you can moan about something bad – to a friend – and save about £60 an hour.

I try hard to describe the taste of pork scratchings, but the best I can come up with is 'delightfully grim': like eating a scale model of Frinton.

Why buy pork scratchings? Well, they're hard to make yourself. I looked it up. If I wanted to, I would have to buy a baby pig, name it, raise it till it was plump, slaughter it, slice it up, then separate and render down the rind in a low oven to produce what's called 'pork dripping'. Then I would have to take the remaining rind, put it back in the oven at a high temperature and cook it until it was crispy. I would also add heaps of salt.

That's a lot of work, and pretty pointless work at that, since all I really have to do is buy a bag of them at the pub. Snack historians say that pork scratchings have been around since the turn of the century. If they are referring specifically to the ones sold in the King and Queen, they are probably right. Mine look like hardened strips of brown matter, dried and fragmented into little shards that could remove a tooth. They are pure cholesterol, but I cannot stop eating them.

In America, no one would dare buy a bag of pork scratchings, unless it was for some weird, ironic party where everyone was supposed to bring them. I buy pork scratchings because I genuinely find them nourishing and fun to look at. Some people might disagree, but I find people who judge food by their looks to be no different from people who judge people by their looks. I call them food racists, or rather, just racists in general. If you don't like pork scratchings, you probably also hate foreigners.

44. THE BATH

It's Sunday afternoon, and I've just woken up. It's about 3 p.m., and it's nearly dark outside – a typical dreary-looking day. I'm already feeling miserable because I've squandered a whole day, and yet here I am watching the end of an omnibus of some soap opera in my underwear, or 'pants', as you fondly call them. I am sitting here, drinking milky tea, wondering if I can salvage anything from the day. Surely there is something I can do that's constructive.

I know. I'll take a bath.

The last time I took a bath was when I was twelve. I had just returned from two weeks of summer camp – a profound nightmare punctuated by fits of crying and diarrhoea. When I finally got home I stripped down in my bedroom and realized I had brought some friends with me. Worms. I had to take a bath. I can remember that bath because in America we stop taking baths around the age of four. As soon as we can stand, we're instructed to use the shower. If anyone found out you were still taking a bath at twelve, you'd be beaten, probably with soap on a rope. Any male past the age of ten who still takes baths usually ends up mutilating cats by the time he's eighteen.

So when I moved to London I was alarmed to find that grown men took baths. Not only did they take them, they talked about them.

Me: 'What did you do last night?'

Kerin: 'Bought the paper, opened a bottle of wine . . . and had a bath.'

Me: 'What?!'

Kerin: 'What What?'

Me: 'A bath? You're thirty-five years old.'

Kerin: 'And you're a twat.'

Many British men, apparently, take (or 'have') baths, and they almost always take them on Sundays. Now I do the very same thing, realizing bathing is by far more fun than showering. Here's why: if you have wasted your day and you can't be bothered to salvage it with a jog around the block or doing laundry, a bath seems like a 'thing to do'. It's better than doing nothing – even if it's just doing nothing submerged in water. You can drink while you're doing it. This is the real reason I believe Brits choose bathing over showering. You can't shower while holding a glass of Merlot. You would ruin the wine, and probably slip and fall and crack your head open. No one would find you for days, so you'd probably be dead and naked – an embarrassing way to go, especially if there's porn nearby. Also, there's the issue of the weather. British weather patterns make the act of showering redundant. Why would you take a shower when it's already raining outside?

I have a bath for one reason only: it helps me slow down the pace of life. It's one of the few times where I can actually do nothing, because sitting in water makes it really hard to do anything else. You cannot repair a toaster or put together a scale model of an Alfa Romeo TZ J. Rolland-G. Augias Coupe des Alpes. I have tried, and the glue just won't hold. What a bath does is remind me how valuable it is to step out of the drive to be productive – something I rarely did in America. I am sure the first time an American man had a bath, another man figured out how to do it better.

45. SHITCUNT

I've been living in London for some time, and I have not yet been to a football match. Clearly, something is wrong with me. If I am to understand the true meaning of life – at least for British men – surely I need to gain a better understanding of the 'beautiful game', the one thing every male in England obsesses over. Really, to have gone a whole season without going to the football is almost shameful. It's akin to going to a whorehouse and spending your time doing sudoku.

Now, here is my first opportunity: Tony, the head of the mail-room, has invited me to see his favourite team, Millwall, play. Tony is a very friendly guy, a pleasant surprise since he's a scary-looking man with a shaven head. He looks like he eats porcupines for breakfast. I am told by friends that this is a typical Millwall supporter. I accept the invitation, knowing that I will be in good hands. Hands that could crush Mondeos.

Now that I've informed a few friends at work of my plans I'm beginning to regret my decision. They've told me I will get my head kicked in, surely, before I even make it to the stadium. Before the match I am fed so many horror stories about hooligan behaviour that I consider wearing body armour (at least a can of all-day breakfast shoved into my pants). I suppose this is what Brits call a 'wind-up'. Everyone knows I'm nervous, so they feed my anxiety with more tales of hooligan terror.

This makes me very nervous, and when I'm nervous, I drink. Prior to the match, Tony, myself and a few others hit a Wetherspoons, a huge chain that serves pints on the cheap. It's about as American as a British pub can be. I can still smell the place on my shirt.

Watching Tony drink pints is equivalent to watching an alligator snatch a deer off dry land; it's a smooth action, accomplished in a single movement. Tony downs a pint in three gulps. I spend thirty minutes nursing mine. I can tell I am being judged. I drink like a Yank. And as I get lapped by fellow drinkers on their fourth, fifth and sixth pint, I realize it's time to switch to vodka.

The fixture is against QPR, which apparently stands for Queens Park Rangers. Even the teams in England have colourful names. Our American teams are much more straightforward: Giants, Jets, Rams. Queens Park Rangers sound like a group of foresters in drag. I ask Tony where Queens Park Rangers play, and he says Queens Park Rangers' ground. Of course.

As we walk to the stadium, located somewhere around an oddly named place called White City, I notice there are far more people on horseback than on foot. These guys are all cops and they look pretty intimidating up there, staring down with their shields and batons. I've never been a fan of horses. I tend to favour gazelles, ostriches and puffins. The crowd grows larger and more vocal as we get closer to the ground. I get nervous as I see men and women downing cans of lager and singing songs. They seem menacing to me because I don't understand the words. I keep thinking of pirates, and it makes me feel better. Remember: 'Drunken football fans are just pirates.'

Drinking in the street always makes events seem a little scarier and unpredictable; it suggests that society's screws have loosened and anarchy is imminent. Anything goes, including public urination, which I see plenty of. I try not to stare. But when they're aiming at your shoes, it's hard not to.

As I continue on my way towards the ground, a little blond kid with his dad walks up beside me. I am talking to Tony and, upon hearing my accent, the kid looks up at me and smiles. 'Fuck off,' he says. I look down at him, and then up at his dad, who seems kind of proud.

There is no drinking allowed during the game, which is good because we are already all drunk. I am the drunkest of them all, because I am the only American – a lightweight among the heavies.

We stand for the entire game, and the beer slowly wears off as the urge to pee grows stronger. People seem genuinely friendly and, twenty minutes into the game, I start to think that all the crap I have been warned about Millwall games is just that: crap. Until the referee makes a bad call.

Then I learn a new word, which is actually two words. It isn't uttered by a hooligan, but by a woman in her fifties wearing a nice dress. She is standing behind me when she yells the immortal expletive: 'Shitcunt.' Then she hollers it again, this time louder than before. It goes quiet, as if she has summoned a mass of agreeable demons. Then I start hearing the phrase reverberate around me. 'SHITCUNT! SHITCUNT! SHITCUNT!'

It starts with a dozen or so men. Then it grows to a hundred . . . then thousands! In America, if anyone did this they'd be escorted out of the grounds, arrested, and immediately enrolled in an anger management course designed specifically for people who say 'shitcunt'. I am speechless.

Until I start to yell, 'Shitcunt!'

If there's one contribution to western culture that the Brits should be proud of, it's legitimizing 'cunt' as a response for everything. And because of this, I have learned to love swearing all over again, especially the word cunt, which I always hated. I now love calling people cunts. I love calling myself a cunt. I would call my mum a cunt but she would probably cry. In fact, I think it's common practice here to call only men 'cunts', and not women. At least that's been my experience, but I could stand to be corrected on this.

Cunt, cunt, cunt, cunt, CUNT! (Sorry, I just saw that kid who swore at me earlier walk by.)

The game ends in a Millwall loss. Or is it a tie? I don't know what the hell is going on. I am a mess. We wander out of the ground, eyeing the cops on horseback, and I'm not entirely sure what happens next because I believe it involves alcohol.

What a relief! I haven't seen a single fight. The closest thing to an act of aggression I've witnessed was when a large group of men singled out another man across the pitch, and chanted about how ugly his white jumper was. It didn't seem to hurt his feelings much, but it was an ugly sweater (and so last year!) and I'm sure he won't be wearing it again any time soon.

But at least he didn't die over it, and that's got to be a good thing.

Compared to US sports, so-called football violence in the UK is a joke. Before the match I witnessed a lot of talk, but no action. In America, all the violence takes place after the game, and it's usually engaged in by thugs who get off on that sort of thing. Meaning the players.

I'm back at the flat, watching TV, and there's a show on about football violence. It's narrated by an ageing magazine editor, and it features guest commentary from other magazine editors and a tough guy soap actor who may or may not be dating another tough guy soap opera actor.

The subject is football rioting, and a few of these older, pudgier 'blokes' are reminiscing about the fun they had in their twenties. Fun, as in bashing each other's heads in.

'It's all crap,' says Dave, a pal who assures me most of these guys did more posturing than punching, and now they're on the telly, they're simply exaggerating their own place in a history that's less real than it is imagined. One guy gets punched and two decades later there are a hundred men taking credit for it.

46. SHOWER GEL

It's Monday, and I'm at my desk. Slowly each staffer wanders in from the tiny elevator, past the copy machine and the reception desk, to take their place in front of their messy workstations. In front of their computers are empty bottles of beer, still there from the final hours of Friday. They remind everyone how short and unremarkable the weekend really is.

The heads of the employees quietly bob as they make their way to the desks. They drop their backpacks or manbags, disengage their iPods and then bring their screens to life. Words are not spoken. I look at Martin, the tall skinny one. Then here comes Nick, the shy one. Then Jimi, the young one. And Dave, the sickly one. They appear to be spent vessels, shaky from two nights of bad pills and dodgy coke, broke from two nights of crawling from pub to club desperately trying to get numbers from girls wearing thick belts and not much else.

But someone says, 'So, how was your weekend?' and the fun begins. It starts with, 'We went to the pub', then moves to, 'I made a phone call', followed by, 'We headed back to my place', and ends with, 'She threw up in the bin'.

I can almost feel the urine slopping around in my shoes, as one lad describes how on Friday night he had sex in the toilets of a grungy pub.

'It was disgusting. There wasn't even a door and the toilet had flooded.'

Still, he describes it like he climbed Everest.

Dave looks over to Martin, a lanky twenty-eight-year-old with floppy hair, who's quietly typing away at his keyboard.

'What'd you get up to?' Dave asks.

'Not much really,' Martin replies. 'I masturbated using shower gel and I didn't even come,' he adds.

He doesn't seem broken up by the result.

Martin's life isn't really that rotten, though. He just likes to paint it that way. Because he knows, like most Brits, that self-loathing is the key to getting laid. I firmly believe that Martin's penchant for painting himself a sexual failure actually gets him more sex than anyone else on the team. Or in the building, for that matter. It's a secret British strategy: the more you play down your luck, the more likely you'll get lucky. The sex you get may be out of pity, but it's still sex, and it counts.

Here are some things I know:

- Men love to play up their sexual achievements in the US.
- Men usually play down their achievements in the UK.
- Australians can't be trusted.

In America, I see bumper stickers on the backs of cars belonging to proud parents, proclaiming how smart their child is. Crap like, 'Grade A Student' or 'Member of the Honor Roll'. I never see these in the UK. But I wonder what they'd be like if they existed. Given the British nature for downplay, I think they would read: 'I Have the Fattest Child in Town' and 'My Daughter's a Slag'.

There is one man in the office who loves to brag about women. I just spent twenty minutes listening to him describe how he had sex with this D-lister on a balcony, bending her over the railing and hiking up her skirt. She's a model and, 'You'd know her if you saw her,' he tells me. When he's done with the story I stand there awkwardly. I get the feeling I've just experienced an American remake of a British film.

At the pub, David is telling a horrible tale.

'And I woke up and she's on top of me . . . and she's big. I'm trying to fight her off, but I'm too drunk. She presses her breasts against my face and puts my willy in her mouth, but it's not working so she gets off me and collapses on the floor. I felt like I was raped by an oompa loompa.'

Eoin tells me about his friend who, after sex, pooped on the satisfied girl's forehead when he only meant to fart. He also ran away. But later, they got married.

Something to note: I admire the low expectations of British women. They put up with everything, including faeces.

All these stories of sex end in some sort of catastrophe. And as revolting as the details may be, they serve to illustrate the true charm of the British male. Here is a creature that stumbles through his sex life, wreaking havoc on women and furniture alike, yet is still able to pull a new girl every weekend. I assume there's a connection here: the ability to reveal their own imperfections makes them instantly more appealing to women than the man on a mission to impress. This is why, whenever British males come to America, they get laid like crazy. Women find them fallible, and more easily approachable. Just don't crap on their foreheads.

47. THE CORNER SHOP

This is the longest period of time I've gone without getting bronchitis. Even during a hard winter, I never coughed up a thimble of phlegm. It has to be London. Back in New York I got bronchitis every month. But here's the weird thing: I am now smoking like a fiend, far more than I did in the US.

I owe it all to these ten packs – the kind I am buying right now at the corner shop on Great Titchfield Street, across from the pub. They cost about as much as a twenty pack in the States, but I don't care. They're so damn adorable, proving my rule that if you put anything in a smaller package it appears significantly more fetching. It's why vile estate agents drive Mini Coopers. Because even they know that Hitler was a cute baby.

I bought my first pack simply because I found them so attractive. I wanted to tickle them like a little kitten (a kitten I could smoke). But more importantly, by buying only ten instead of twenty, I felt like I was doing myself a favour. Right now, for example, as I slip the pack into my pocket, I'm telling myself that it's not only healthier than purchasing a twenty pack, it's healthier than not smoking at all!

Take, for example, the warnings one finds on the packaging. I love them because they're far more direct and brutal than anything you'd find on a pack of Parliaments stateside. The pack I have now has a very simple warning: 'Smoking causes impotence', which actually seems more alarming than my previous favourite, 'Smoking kills'. In the US, the warning runs over three or four sentences and mentions the 'Surgeon General'. As a deterrence, this works about as well as a G-string on a stripper. It's only there temporarily as a mild distraction.

'Smoking kills'. I like that one because it reminds me that my time on this planet is merely temporary, and I should enjoy every single drag of that cigarette before snubbing it out. So, in a weird way, the warnings have the opposite effect of their intention. I now smoke more than ever. And I love every minute of it. When they banned smoking in New York bars, I watched my habit dwindle to a few cigs a day. I hate social engineering, but at least in this case the benefits were clear. I could now go up a flight of stairs without seeing a bright white light and hearing my great-grandmother beckoning me towards it.

Now I smoke more, and I have never felt healthier. Perhaps it's because I enjoy smoking more than ever; there is nothing better than smoking in a pub – a luxury banned in Manhattan, and, in time, it will be banned here too. Could it be that the happiness brought on by a pint and a smoke elevates certain chemicals in my body that offset the harm brought on by my smoking and drinking?

I would say yes. I am currently smoking as I head to my flat. Right now anyway, in England, I can smoke in bars, restaurants, cafes and, if I'm sly, church. You can smoke while you're buying smokes! How cool is that?

I am almost home, but I should stop at the King's Arms. It's lovely and empty at this time of the day (3:30 p.m.). Yes, I'm drinking more too. Not in quantity, but in frequency. Living in Manhattan, drinking came in binges. I'd stay dry for two days then go off the deep end as a reward. It was a horrible way to live – inconsistency breeds a moodiness that puts you always on edge. I prefer my life now: I drink almost every night, but only a few pints before I get tired and wander home or into a park. But oddly, sometimes I will drink just so I can smoke.

Brits seem to relish their smoking and they do it everywhere. Even non-smokers smoke, simply by inhaling deeply in pubs.

'Passive smokers should buy their own,' Chris tells me, as we plough through a pack, staring at a non-smoking couple in the corner.

Smoking is fun. And because it's fun, Brits do it. Brits are more interested in having fun than growing old . . . and maybe that's why everyone here looks so old. And the reason why everyone here looks old is because they *are* old. And they are old because they aren't dead. They aren't dead, because happiness, brought on by drinking and smoking, protects them from illness. If they were dead, they wouldn't be sitting around drinking and smoking – which says a lot about the wondrous effects of drinking and smoking.

If this makes sense to you, then you have been drinking.

48. OVEN CLEANER

Dave just called. He's not coming into work tomorrow. He cleaned his oven. He did this without wearing gloves and now he's come down with some crazy disease that's eating away at his hands. He meets me at the pub, and he shows them to me. They are red, puffy and swollen, and it seems sadly ironic that his hands appear to look like oven mitts.

The doctors can't figure out what it is, so now he's gone to a holistic doctor who told him to bathe his limbs in some Chinese stinky herbs. Now he's back with the doctor, who's given him steroids. They've done wonders, and the skin is clearing up. The bad news is he's gone completely muscle-bound. His chest has grown into a barrel, and it appears this little man could bench press a Vauxhall.

Brits get funny diseases. They seem almost fictional, like something out of a book by Dickens, and almost always involving nasty eruptions on the skin. I'd never seen a boil until I came here. I saw a woman with one on her neck. It had its own scarf.

My theory on wellness has changed a bit since I moved here. In America, when I was sick I would go to the doctor, get some pills, and whatever was wrong with me would clear up over four days. But the next time I got sick with the same thing, it was almost always worse. In England, you are never really told what you have, so you rarely get any medicine. Instead, you go home and drown yourself in tea and Benylin and watch reruns of *The Office* until your retinas bleed. Then you go to the doctor for that, and repeat the whole cycle.

My British doctor doesn't tell me much. I get the idea that English doctors are about as touchy-feely as a thumbscrew. That's good, in my opinion, since overly friendly doctors always end in misery. Friendly doctors get stuff wrong. That's why they're friendly. They have to rely on 'bedside manner' because, as their patient, you almost always end up bedridden. They're really good at explaining that everything's going to be fine, up to the point you're dead. American doctors are great, but they're always trying to help, and sometimes they cause more harm than good. British doctors are OK I think, but only if they do absolutely nothing.

Dave is back in the office, and he's wearing black tape over his fingertips because they hurt when he types. He's off the steroids because they're too powerful, and now the strange affliction has returned. I feel bad for him, of course, so I decide he might need to see someone more qualified than his current physician.

We go to the pub.

49. THE STONE ROSES

There are more than a dozen pubs in my neighbourhood, and by now I've figured out who goes where. The Goths go to the theme pub on Wells Street, the women with prams go to the gastropub on Foley Street, and the coked-up divorcees hit the wine bar on Dean Street. I go to the empty pubs with bad carpeting. I like empty pubs because in them I find people like me who prefer empty pubs. I like the King and Queen. It's never crowded and the people seem every bit as antisocial as me. The only aberration is the strange-looking folk music club that meets upstairs every Monday evening. They are a frightening-looking group, snaking up to the first floor of the pub around 6 p.m., carrying oddly shaped cases containing instruments no one plays any more. I imagine they'll be reciting Shakespearean sonnets upstairs while plucking on a zither. I try not to make eye contact as they move by us. They have an air of superiority about them. Somehow, I blame Bob Dylan for this.

A group of us are currently sitting around a middle table, on our third or fourth round, and big opinions about small things are starting to take shape. More precisely, an argument over the Stone Roses. Vic, sitting across to me, maintains they were the greatest British band ever. To my right, Dave points out that they only put out a few records, and only one of them 'wasn't shit'. Dave thinks the only group that truly matters is Radiohead, the delightfully upbeat band that are strangely derivative of the Monkees.

I feel like I've been here before. In America, we call this 'high school'. But then I remind myself that I experienced this same argument last week, around the same time. It's called the Stone Roses vs. Radiohead argument.

I've never heard much of the Stone Roses. They never made it big in America, but to some young men in Britain they are God-like, the greatest, and they're always fodder for passionate conversation. Passionate annoying conversation. I am convinced the Stone Roses existed primarily to instigate heartfelt, nearly violent arguments as to why they are the greatest band ever. It's a band that exists not to listen to, but to fight about.

The 'who's a better band' argument is the staple of a pub night – a conversation that never happens in America, because we simply don't care enough beyond our own problems to discuss the merits of some band. In a British pub, if you were talking about any band, whether the Beatles or the Bees, some guy would inevitably mutter, 'They aren't the Stone Roses.' Actually, if you were talking about groundbreaking medical procedures, whether it was coronary artery bypass grafts, balloon angioplasty or a vasectomy, some guy would inevitably mutter, 'It's not as good as the Stone Roses.'

I love this. In the US, we don't have pub arguments because we don't have arguments. When Yanks fight, there has to be a foreseeable conclusion. Not so here. Arguments are there to fuel more arguing, so you can drink more. The drinking facilitates more arguing, until you get so drunk you can't say 'facilitate' any more.

The argument here at the pub is almost over. How can I tell? It's easy. It's when the only word you keep hearing from one of the combatants is 'bollocks'. Vic is now saying 'bollocks' repeatedly. He has been ganged up on by three mates ripping him on the Stone Roses' second record. I realize now that waiting for an argument in a pub to end is like waiting for your microwave popcorn to be ready. Simply replace the popping noise with 'bollocks'. The 'bollocks' start slowly, then by the fourth minute they reach a heightened intensity before trailing off into a 'bollocks' every third second. That means the argument is just about over.

For pub arguments to work, though, I think there can be no workplace hierarchy. At the pub it always disappears. Right now, for example, a work experience boy who's only been on the job for a week just insulted me over my terrible British impersonation. That never would have happened in America, I think, as I sit quietly nursing my wound. The Oxbridge-educated little prick seems pleased with himself, even when I fire him.

Pub arguments can be tedious but they beat heart to heart conversations hands down. I've been in England for two years, and I've yet to have one of those. No one has ever sat me down to tell me their problems. With the exception of these loud fights over bands, most people keep their feelings locked up. This is fine by me. I don't need to hear it. Give me this 'stiff upper lip' any day.

In America, there are no quiet people, except for the ones that end up shooting twenty kids in a school. In the US, you always hear a killer described as a 'quiet' person. Does that mean everyone in the UK is a secret homicidal maniac? I'm thinking there are fewer attention-seekers in the UK, meaning there's no guy trying to be the life of the party when a photo is taken. Instead, I notice pictures are only taken after someone is passed out drunk, and only after he is covered with shaving cream and condiments. I've learned never to pass out in a roomful of Brits, because only then will YOU be the centre of attention. It took me a week to shit out that glue stick.

And so the Stone Roses argument ends in a stand-off, with both combatants calling each other cunts, over and over again. I suddenly feel something warm against my leg. It's a small dog. I hope.

50. PUB DOGS

Just yesterday, while trying to dodge traffic, I stumbled upon a monument located near Hyde Park. It read: 'THE ANIMALS IN WAR MEMORIAL. They had no choice. This memorial is dedicated to animals who served and died alongside British and Allied forces in wars and campaigns throughout time.' A monument like that would never exist in the USA, nor would you find a planter with a plaque that reads: 'Metropolitan Drinking Fountain and Cattle Trough Association'. Because no such association exists in America. England is a land of strange organizations, bizarre priorities and funny plaques. I have learned to keep my eyes open, because you never know what you'll sit on or step in.

Like this small dog rubbing up against my calf.

Small dogs seem to be everywhere, and like tonight, in pubs. Pub dogs are usually tethered to old men with white hair. You can't get to the toilets without stepping on a panting mat of flea-ridden hair (which is often the owner, not the dog).

Weirdly, they never bark, not even when you kick them. This is strange: English dogs don't bark. In the US, that's all you hear at night. I wonder if maybe British dogs have their vocal cords removed when they're puppies. Or, could it be that the owners have actually taught their pets the 'stiff upper lip'?

I look down at the dog – it's a terrier, and for once it's nice to see a creature on all fours in a bar that isn't me. I suppose the pub dog symbolizes what's wonderful about England: inclusion. Walk into any pub and you may find a twenty-two-year-old secretary, a forty-five-year-old man with one leg, a ninety-year-old retired postman, a bucket of crabs, and a mangy West Highland terrier sniffing someone's crotch.

At first I thought it strange that someone would actually take their dog drinking. But now it makes perfect sense: it's a cheap date. And it's not like the mutt knows the difference between Carling and Boddingtons. He also won't complain about choosing '99 Luftballons' on the jukebox. In UK pubs, pets are always welcome, probably in order to help drinkers avoid the stigma of drinking alone. Entering a pub with your dog might even make others believe you're there because the dog wanted to go. But now this dog has moved on, and I digress. The glasses are empty and everyone seems to be staring at me. Quietly. Oh yes, it's my turn to buy the round.

51. THE ROUND

Buying rounds is fun, especially when it's not your turn. But it is my turn, so I'd better get up. It's a pleasure to pay, especially when you know you've got a pint coming later. The feeling you get when someone stands up and says 'My round' is not unlike the emotion one feels when finding money down the back of the sofa, or your last pair of clean underwear.

Buying rounds is an exercise in egalitarianism that, for once, actually works. Everyone pays, no matter how wealthy or poor. Even better: women pay, a practice seldom seen in the US. It's pretty refreshing not to have to buy a girl a drink, especially when you notice she's spent five hundred bucks on her shoes.

Buying rounds prevents assholes from getting out of paying and suckers from paying too much. No one gets away with not buying a round – if you're broke, you have to say you're broke, which everyone is happy to hear anyway because they're probably broke too. In England, the worst thing you can say about anyone is 'he doesn't stand his round'. Remember that the next time it's your turn.

I am learning the maths of drinking. If there are five people at a table, then that night you will have five drinks. Five people means five rounds, and that means five drinks each. So it's less about generosity, and more about getting what's yours. Which is five drinks. It's a sort of imbibe-able socialism, which may be the only socialism that actually works.

You know when you buy the first round (always the best round to buy, since you appear less cheap and there's a possibility that more people might join your group later), you are guaranteed four in return. It's basically money in the bank. This also works with six, seven and even eight people. Although when the group gets larger it's often better to split into separate rounds, to prevent everyone from going broke or getting angry because somebody got left out.

Another thing I just learned tonight: never send a woman to take an order for more than four drinks. Someone's girlfriend just went to the bar with an order and came back with something else entirely. I ordered a vodka and soda, and whatever she's brought me has something with an umbrella in it.

But that problem pales to the one I'm dealing with now. I've still not managed to drink as quickly as the Brits, and the folks I'm with tonight drink faster than I pee. I'm way behind with my pint, which means I will miss out on a round, while everyone else loads up. I need to drink faster, I tell myself, but it's impossible. Pints are big things; I never can get to the bottom of one before that last half-inch has gone warm. Eoin has necked a pint in three gulps, meaning I have to buy him another while I'm still holding a full one. This is not fair.

I am amazed as I watch British women, like my friend Jenni, down booze like it's air. The sheer quantity of booze British women can drink is positively astounding, and to be admired, I think. Until they piss themselves, which is a common sight, usually near my apartment.

Eoin has just swallowed another pint in two gulps. He has lapped me yet again, on his fourth pint while I am on my second. That's it. I give up. No more pints. Now I'm drinking rosé wine. When I drink it, it's like tequila – I always walk into trees.

I am ridiculed for drinking rosé. A man isn't supposed to drink a pink wine, I'm told by Eoin, mid-gulp into his fifth pint. But what do I care? I was just at the bar, and bought the round, and I didn't have to say 'Keep the change'. That's nice. You pay for your drinks, and you don't even have to tip. That means I have extra change for the cigarette machine. Jenni scrapes together about three pounds and I give her another £2.50 needed for a pack of Marlboro Lights. There are only sixteen smokes in a pack designed for twenty. This makes no sense to me, but it still beats not smoking at all.

I look at the clock, and we've got thirty minutes before closing. I decide to order another 'quick one', a small glass of rosé, and down it quickly. And so it's time to leave. I walk outside and into a tree.

52. COBRA EXTRA SMOOTH PREMIUM DOUBLE FILTERED LAGER

On the morning of 7 July 2005 I have a meeting with my boss and a few other serious men in suits at the Cleveland Street building. As we are looking at numbers on a wall (our declining sales), we get word from an arriving co-worker that the tube has been hit by madmen with bombs. We stop talking for a moment and instinctively look out of the window. Whenever bad stuff hits, people always look out of windows. I feel a cold sweat coming over me, and then the inevitable memory of 9/11. That morning in 2001 I was hung over and passed out in my Hell's Kitchen apartment when I heard the sirens. I had no idea what was going on, because I was too wasted to investigate.

Now, in my office in London, work resumes. We continue with our meeting – stuff involving charts and spreadsheets. My boss, Bruce, loves charts and spreadsheets. He looks at them the way the rest of us look at porn.

As the meeting continues, I think it strange that people can do this: act as though nothing has happened. In my head I'm going nuts but Bruce just keeps acting like Bruce: a calm, robotic voice, as even as a congenial dial tone. Of course, no one is pretending that nothing's happened – they're just 'getting on with it', a phrase I hear over and over again in England. 'Getting on with it' is the refusal to let horrible things stop you from doing what you're supposed to do. It's something the Brits are very good at, along with drinking. Which begins, in earnest, after the meeting ends.

After accounting for everyone on the team, we return to our desks while the rest of the staff gather around a television in the newsroom to hear the worst from an awful day. It seems only appropriate that I send people home, but no one leaves – mainly because all the train lines are down and we have lots of beer in the fridge.

So now I am back at my desk, drinking Cobra Extra Smooth Premium Doubled Filtered lager. It's from India. We got a case sent to us from some PR company, and we're all drinking it. I was going to go to the gym, but now I'm not. Life is too short, but more importantly, I am too drunk. Fuck the gym. Terrorism is another reason not to go to the gym. I might not even shower; screw those bastards!

Here's the strange thing: With the exception of the bombs and the carnage, everything is fine here. Bombs go off around the corner and the Brits do what they do best: they go to the pub and get drunk and make the best of it. Even better, the cricket is still going on (that's a game played by tall men in white pants. A single game can last several years). My managing editor, Eoin – you know, the guy with 'Millwall' tattooed on the inside of his lower lip – says, 'We fought Hitler! It'll take a bit more than some shits with carrier-bag bombs on a tube to put us off. It was a bit of a piss-poor effort. Shall we have another pint then?'

We do have another pint, and 'a laugh'. And then 'a wee'. Eoin has big, caring arms.

You Brits are obviously used to this terrorist crap, what with the IRA, and I suppose you pride yourselves on carrying on as if nothing has happened. It's actually very cool. Everyone here is scared, but no one shows any fear. That's a British thing. You are tough little bastards. There's no question that everyone feels bad about what's happened, but no one is letting that interfere with their resolve, or their drinking. They figure the enemy should be the ones who are scared, not them, which is always the way to think, I reckon. I love these people. They aren't like the Spanish.

After draining the fridge of beer, we head out to the King and Queen, which is packed to the gills. Mel, the excitable landlord, is frantically busy.

'I hate to say it,' he says, cradling a mass of just-emptied pint glasses, 'but this is great for business.'

He's absolutely right, the lovable bastard. I drink there for a while, and realize I'm the only American in the bunch. It doesn't much matter to anyone but me, probably.

All around the area, the pubs are packed and everyone is getting shit-faced. We left the office around noon, and now it's about 10 p.m. or so, and people are trying to find their way home. Some are staying out all night. Others are planning the long walk home because there's still no tube service. It's a perfect night for it. I slip out of another pub and stumble back to the office to see if anyone's around. I am now back at my desk, alone and feeling woozy. Most of my staff have left for better places, to get drunker or to get laid. Sitting here now, I'm thinking of ordering some Indian food. Maybe chicken tikka masala or tandoori chicken or maybe lamb korma. I could probably get a mixed grill. Something that has a little of everything. Perhaps some keema naan thrown in? Why not! Screw those bastards!

53. THE OFFICE RERUNS ON UKTV GOLD

I can always count on one thing being on TV when I get home from the pub: *The Office*. There's an episode on every day, on every channel, at every hour. Christ, I love the show, but they've made only twelve episodes, and I've seen them all at least one hundred times. It's no longer a joy to see – it's become background noise as common as gas from grandma.

The Office is on mainly late at night, and for good reason. When nothing else is on and you're drunk, it's the default choice – a comfortable pillow to rest your brain when you can't be bothered with the hard steely logic behind a cooking show.

But for me, *The Office* also serves as an education, revealing a key difference in the way British and American men communicate. In the very first scene of the first series, Ricky Gervais's character David Brent attempts to make a point about the type of boss he is by creating an imagined, hypothetical conversation. He is interviewing a man for a fork-lift driving position. Instead of addressing the man sitting directly in front of him with questions about qualifications, he fabricates a conversation between himself and the applicant.

It's funny, but for an American it's also pretty confusing, because somewhere within one short speech the character has switched points of view – from himself, to the applicant, and then to himself again. It's hard to follow, like tailing Jason Bourne through Tangiers.

I have never seen anyone talk like this in the US, on television or in real life. But I see it every day at work. Here is a typical example where a Brit adopts two different voices, by my friend Chris, who is explaining a hypothetical conversation:

'So, we're in the pub, and Martin says he's seen, online, this video of a minor member of the Royal Family sucking off a horse.'

'You what, Martin?'

'I absolutely swear it, mate, no lie.'

'A horse?'

'A big one.'

'What, a member of the royal family?'

'Absolutely. Giving a stallion a proper blowjob. Big time.'

'I mean, what an idiot. Utter bollocks.'

Even more unusual to the American ear, however, is that the actual conversation never takes place, but is instead brought up to make a point that's favourable to the person talking. Chris is implying that Martin is full of shit, and always talking nonsense. But Chris, being kind-hearted, would never say that. Instead he creates a hypothetical conversation about a royal giving a horse a blowjob.

I think a psychologist would call it a 'discursive multiple-personality affectation' or something like that. I would call it 'nuts'.

Why do Brits seem to be the only people who do this?

Firstly, I think it's because they like doing impressions of each other. An awful lot of British humour is based on nothing more than very accurate impersonation (Borat, Alan Partridge, Jeremy Paxman). Secondly, unlike Yanks, Brits are less forthright and have serious issues with coming out directly and saying, 'Yes, I'm right, and you're wrong.' To avoid bragging, you need to remove it by one step at least, through a complicated exercise using a fictitious conversation. Every Brit, therefore, briefly becomes a skilled novelist, albeit briefly with a spasm of Dickens. Not only does it work, it's highly entertaining – for me, anyway.

But it's late and I'm starting to doze on the sofa. Oh wait . . . another episode of *The Office* is on, this time on UKTV Gold! And it's the one with the Dance! I haven't seen that one since it was on thirty minutes earlier on Channel Four.

54. HEN PARTIES

Elena, myself, and my visiting drunken American friend Bill are waiting at King's Cross for my friends from work, Jenni and Dave. We're taking a train to Brighton, to watch three of my male employees 'perform' at a hen night in a dingy nightclub. As part of a story assignment, Nick, Martin and Jimi are to do an entire striptease in front of a rabid group of drunk, horny and aggressive women – revealing their assortment of penises to all. This is one of the perks of my job: forcing people to do things that I would find terrifying.

Jenni shows up with a bag of alcohol containing half a dozen or so bottles of various vodkas and gins, which she promptly drops when she sees us, shattering them into a leaky mess by the entrance. We hop the train and head to Brighton, unfortunately sober.

We find the club – a cheesy dank armpit of a building that smells of basement rot. We enter and find hundreds of sweaty girls in various states of drunkenness weaving around screaming and shouting, many wearing bunny ears. I am told by the manager that tonight's performers are in the back, in the 'dressing room'. I push myself through the throng, amazed that despite the weight of some of these girls they can still fit themselves into miniskirts.

The bar is called the Babylon Lounge, a purpose-built, pack-'em-in bar/club on the seafront. It looks like a big DIY barn on some forgotten industrial estate. The strip group appearing that night is called Adonis Cabaret, run by a man called Tristan – a 'lovely' guy, as you say, and surprisingly straight.

The event is a classic British night out, one of the strippers, Nick, explains to me, in that every belief held by a foreigner of the British being cultured, sophisticated and urbane would crumble before their eyes like so much washed-away beer vomit if they could see it. Most people are ugly when drunk, but British women excel at it – they do leering, groping, shouting and puking like no one else on earth. These girls are ten times scarier than men in a similar condition, because they're smart enough to know that they're less likely to be punched in the face if they try to push you out of the way at the bar/steal your drink/shove their hand into your pants/empty a handbag full of sick on to your table.

I am at the back of the club, up a few steps from the main floor where the girls are congregating. I find a buffet – a few cardboard tables stacked with stale vegetables, chicken wings and something that may or may not be meat balls. I try one. Still, no definitive answer. I see the manager – a nice-looking gentleman who also happens to be a male stripper. I ask him where the dressing room is, and he points me to a narrow door which appears to be an entrance to an electrical closet. Because it is.

I open the door and find my three employees naked and huddled together in a cupboard filled with exposed wiring and genitalia. Each one of them is gripping a porno mag, feverishly but fruitlessly wanking in order to build up a hard-on. I turn my back quickly and walk out. Nick emerges with something wrapped around him and explains to me that, before they go out, they must first get hard and then apply one of these (he shows me a thick rubber ring) around the base of his erection in order to maintain it while they dance. 'This is not something I regularly do on a night out,' Nick tells me, holding his limp dick.

He returns to the closet, and I look in. I can see all of them are having serious problems. I order them tequila shots.

I move back towards the buffet and have a drink with Elena, Jenni, Bill and Dave. Bill is stumbling a bit, barely holding on to his cigarette. The club is now packed and the women are getting drunker and rowdier. They are chanting, and baying for dancers.

The music starts and the three men burst out of the electrical cupboard, all dressed as firemen. They snake from the back of the club, through the crowd, to the front, as women paw and pull at their clothes. They make the stage and begin their dance, one they apparently choreographed and practised early that morning because it's not half bad. Women – all straight hair, thick belts, bunny ears and beer-stained skirts – attempt to grab at them. It's a frenzy; nothing like I've ever seen in a strip club for men. When a man sees a naked woman, he just sits and stares, downloading visual material to be used later behind a locked bathroom door.

These women, though, are positively rabid . . . dangerous even.

I stand near the buffet and continue stuffing my face. Suddenly a song by Franz Ferdinand comes on and, knowing that this is the climax, I move closer to the throng to see the three gyrating men flip their kits, exposing their semi-rigid members to everyone. The women scream with delight, pawing at the men's legs. Their genitals vary in size and shape, but for some reason Martin's was the most memorable – it resembles a pancake squeezed into the shape of a door knob. Purely by this mutant display he's scaring the hell out of the women.

After the song ends the three flabby men stumble off the stage and struggle their way through the crowd, many of whom are stuffing phone numbers in the dancers' hats and mouths. But as they make their way back to the electrical closet, they are quickly forgotten. Because, on stage now is a large black man, also in a fireman's outfit. I met him earlier – his name is Paul Grant and he has a fourteen-inch penis. I tried to measure it, but my ruler stops at twelve. He can touch his own back with it.

Onstage, Paul quickly drops all of his gear, and reveals a penis so long it is actually fastened to his hip bone. He grabs a bottle of lotion, unfastens his member and spritzes a healthy topping of lotion on it. Then he grabs his dick and waves it around and around like an aeroplane propeller – as hypnotic as it is messy, he sprays the crowd with lotion. Which they lovingly lap up. I am laughing and a little disturbed, until I recognize the tall woman in the front row, shouting affirmatively at the stripper's turgid tentacle. It's my wife. I decide to get her and go drinking.

In the club later, after having performed onstage, the three amateur strippers are treated as micro-celebrities: rival hen groups are scoring points by seeing how many of the three they can have talking to them at once. But despite being apparently all over them, they aren't willing to go beyond flirting. It seems that not even drunken British girls on a night out want other girls to see them snogging a stripper.

I did not know what a hen party was until I came to London. In America, they have 'bachelorette parties', and they're calm affairs. Essentially, a group of women go to dinner and then rent a movie. The height of excitement might be choosing the flavour of the Ben & Jerry's. Boring, true, but it will probably save you a night in the A&E ward.

55. CAR BOOT SALE

It's Sunday, and Elena and I are trying to think of something to do. I call Andy, who's always full of ideas. He immediately suggests we go to a 'car boot sale'. I'm new to using the word 'boot' to describe a trunk, so I don't know what he means.

'Car boot sales are like your garage sales, but instead of doing it at your garage, you load your up car, drive to a field, and sell stuff out of the trunk.'

But just like garage sales, these are now mostly professional operations where people spend the week buying shit (some of it new and somehow hopelessly depressing like mop heads and rubber gloves) and go to the designated field and set up a big table in front of their car and pile on the bric-a-brac.

'These pros also swoop on innocent house-clearing folk like vultures,' Andy says. You turn up in your car with a trunk full of unwanted things and they start tearing at it the minute you get out so they can pay you two quid and then sell it on their own car boot table for three. I explain this to Elena – and how much fun it would be to spend a morning going 'bootfairing'.

'But it sounds like going on eBay,' she says, 'except with rain and mud and smelly people.'

That's why I married her. So we stay home and get drunk instead.

56. WELLIES

It's Monday, and I've come home from work to find Elena standing on the dining room table. She's bent over because she's tall, and her head is hitting the ceiling. She's wearing wellington boots. They're black, with butterflies and flowers on them. She's pointing to the corner where, she says, a mouse is hiding. Of all things, the rodent has retreated underneath a white box that held the wireless mouse for our recently purchased laptop. I kick the box, and the mouse scurries across the floor. Elena screams, and he makes it to the kitchen, where he disappears into a hole under the fridge. Elena refuses to come down until I call pest control.

Wellington boots were invented in Britain to help combat melting snow, heavy showers and the muddy ground it causes on farmland. Now, I think they're worn by women terrified of mice.

And so they should be. British mice seem to be pretty gutsy creatures, unafraid of human life and brazen in their actions. We can be sitting watching the telly and one will zip across the floor oblivious to the curry-eating giants on the couch. I remember reading somewhere of a UK study done on mice, where researchers injected them with amphetamines while forcing them to listen to the Prodigy. The mice that listened to the music at high volumes perished, proving to scientists the deleterious effects of listening to bad music, even for rodents.

So what happened to the mice that survived these cruel studies? I imagine they are living in my flat. Which is why I thank God for wellington boots, for these waterproof rubber galoshes give Elena a sense of immunity, as she now refuses to take them off. She is wearing them right now, in the bedroom. She's probably not alone in this practice, for I would think the boots in black would make excellent fetish gear for experimental couples. And this is why I like British mice, and actually never called pest control.

57. THE SUN AND THE STOCKS

It's around 6 p.m. and I'm walking against foot traffic down High Holborn. As I cross the street of a busy intersection, I run into a knot of traffic, both human and mechanical. Everyone seems hopelessly stuck, confused as to how to move forwards. The cars can't make it through the single lane, and the pedestrians cannot cross. The reason for this: a street sweeper with its lowered high-pressure spray bars has settled for a moment, crawling at a snail's pace, clogging the pedestrian crossing and the path of oncoming traffic. I don't know what to make of it. It's 6 p.m., and the city has decided to clean the streets at the height of rush hour. I am more amazed, however, at the pedestrians, in their suits, they all stand calmly. I suppose they are used to this sort of thing. As the crowd grows larger, stuck on the little cement island, I notice a collective sigh involving roughly 430 people.

The cars don't honk here much. In New York, the man behind the wheel of the street sweeper would already be dead, and his bones turned into delightful key chains to be sold in Times Square. But not so in London, and I assume there's a reason for this. Perhaps street cleaning at rush hour is designed specifically to slow things down. Great Britain, no matter where you are, is a study in pacing. And any time you violate that pace, say, when you try to hurry, something like a street sweeper appears to remind you to knock it off. See, at that moment, I was in a hurry, trying to make an appointment . . . on time! Somehow this was caught on CCTV (there are on average seventy-five cameras on every street – I read that in the *Daily Mail*, next to an article on conjoined turtles), and a street sweeper was dispatched to disrupt the flow. It worked, and now I am going to be late.

Which is fine. This city is designed for people who are late, and to frustrate those who need or expect people to be on time. I almost never arrive anywhere on time any more, even though I already know that wherever I go, whether by foot, taxi or tube, it will take twenty-five minutes to get there. If there is potential for early arrival, you will be stabbed to ensure that doesn't happen.

Delays come in all shapes and sizes. Here I am in a cafe near Chancery Lane, trying to order a quick coffee, but the coffee machine makes 'quick' impossible. Order a small cup of coffee anywhere in the world and a guy simply flips a toggle and out it pours. This does not exist here, in England, where a cup of coffee takes seven angry minutes to trickle from that gleaming silver box, a burbling accompanied by an insidious hiss that mimics a cottonmouth moccasin. I've never heard something work so hard to produce so little. The only thing you can do at this point is sit down and read the paper.

If it wasn't for tabloids I don't know what I would do with my life. I am convinced these papers were created to purposely fill in the spaces of time created by waiting in queues and cafes. Waiting for coffee, I am already through the *Sun*'s marvellous gossip section, and I'm not moving until I get to Dear Deirdre. Sadly, she never runs my letter.

I love the *Sun* for a zillion different reasons, but I know that being an American means I have no immune system to protect myself from the things I read in it. In America we have nothing as interesting or dangerous. Instead, we have *USA Today*, a paint-by-numbers high school rag designed for adults who were dropped on their heads as children. *USA Today* is filled with simple charts and simpleton opinions – a paper written and designed to wrap fish, provided the fish cannot read.

Because I am a tabloid virgin, I believe everything I read in them. This morning, I became engrossed in a section detailing the recent crimes occurring in a local town. Spousal abuse, murder, deadly car accidents – this city was out of control. The reporter included lots of personal details: apparently Tracy is going to tell Mary that she is moving back in with Charlie, even though she is hiding her true feelings. I realized moments later that I was reading the plot summaries of that week's soap operas.

Thanks to the tabloids, though, I now believe the city is overrun by vicious gangs, illegal immigrants, yobs, ASBO-loving teens, hoodies with knives, benefit fraudsters and pregnant teens. I blame this on the repetition of identical stories. One mugging translates into four tabloid stories, told in a remarkably similar way but with a stray new fact or two thrown in. This causes me to believe falsely that in September alone there were over 4.5

million stabbings in Harlesden alone. And they've all been done by the same guy, named Ja'mal.

Because there are far fewer guns available in the UK, the crimes committed here are infinitely more creative, usually involving hammers or ice-picks, as well as the ice-pick/hammer combination. Without the availability of firearms, crimes become far more memorable. In New York, I can't remember who I shot last.

I do think there is more crime in London, though, and the policing and sentencing laws are pretty awful. If you commit a crime, you have a better chance of having sex with the Queen in Holland Park than being arrested. Then, when you're arrested, and you happen to be found guilty, you will serve only a fraction of your time, upon which you will be released to a council flat of your own choosing. You will decorate it with St George's flags. Really, it's just another branch of the vaunted English civil service. I suspect criminals here even get pensions.

I'm sorry. Maybe I long for the good old days of Elizabethan England. I am referring to the stocks. I've always been quite taken with that much maligned invention. The stocks were created in medieval times to restrain and humiliate minor offenders. You'd place the criminal's head and wrists through holes in a board, and then lock the poor sap up. He'd have to endure this punishment in every kind of weather (meaning, usually, rain), and always in a city centre, since public stocks were usually placed in public places.

'You used to be able to go here,' says Kerin, pointing to Marble Arch, 'and throw rotten fruit at people in the stocks. You'd buy a meat pie and some ale and make a day out of it.'

The last recorded use of the stocks was in west Wales, in 1872, but you can also find them at renaissance fairs, where you can get your picture taken in them. Maybe I'm an old fart, but I think it's a shame they aren't being pressed back into service for real. Bringing back the stocks for both England and America would be a great thing. They'd be perfect punishment for Paris Hilton and Britney Spears, as well as George Galloway and people who talk too loudly on their mobile phones at checkout queues.

Oh dear. I seem to have got lost. This always happens when I leave home without a map. Thank God for 'Bobbies'.

58. BOBBIES

I'm supposed to be in Mayfair, and I think I've missed the main road. Thank God for these nice men in the funny hats. They're always happy to give directions. You call them Bobbies, right? They're supposed to be cops, I'm told, but I never see them policing anything. I notice that they're pretty good at giving directions and taking pictures as favours for tourists. Other than that, British cops seem to be about as useful as a birthday party clown, but without the balloon artistry, face painting and the added bonus of a magic show.

Whenever I'm lost, I always ask a cop for directions. Half the time, they're right. The cop I just asked has sent me in a completely wrong direction. I know this because I asked another cop a few yards up the road – also giving directions! – and he pointed me back to where I came from.

The men and women in uniform are always polite and well spoken. They're a lovely luxury in the daytime, but I imagine they aren't much help at night. But at least if you need a photographer, you always have one on call. Bobbies are always happy to take your picture, because it's one of those few things that involve assisting others without actually getting hurt. My friend Paul, an American cop, believes UK criminals are usually better armed than UK cops, so the cops won't put themselves at risk. It's not worth it. And when they don't put themselves at risk, well, that just emboldens the criminals. So what you have are two groups – one consisting of cops happy to take photos, and another who will stab you and take the camera after you've had your picture taken.

Don't get me wrong. I love the cops. I just think they should be allowed guns, and they should be allowed to use them . . . at the very least, on street performers (living statues, primarily). I suppose not having guns is designed to keep the street cops from getting too cocky. But maybe cockiness wouldn't be such a bad thing.

I guess I am getting older. I am beginning to sound that way. I worry about crime, and complain about lack of punishment. I am also urinating more often in the middle of the night. All of this stuff goes hand in hand. My colleagues joke that I have become a *Daily Mail* reader. Is that bad?

My crime-inspired paranoia is only encouraged by my colleagues, however. This morning, one of them called in around 10 a.m. to tell me that his flat had been broken into, and now he can't leave for work until the locksmith comes to repair the door. I get a call like this every week, always from a different employee. Because of this, I assume England is rife with brazen and incredibly busy home-invaders.

'Most of those guys are lying to you,' my friend Ross finally tells me.

He informs me that saying your flat was robbed is a far better reason for missing work than saying you've got the flu or have food poisoning. With a break-in, you don't have to fake a 'sick voice', and you can show up the next day without having to pretend you're recovering. I suppose this is an old trick and, knowing that I'm a naive American, my staff employ it as much as possible. I admire that. I just wished I had learned it when I was younger.

Wow. I sound old. And, it's true, I am. Perhaps I should go to the pub. Maybe I'll buy a little dog first. And watch *Countdown*. I could have biscuits. Oh look, those damn kids are in the street again playing that music. Why do I have to pee so much? Better heat up the kettle. Where's my tea towel? Oh dear.

59. THE BARMAID

Everyone has a gripe with their local. Usually it's a jukebox that features only Wham! or a toilet that smells like Grimsby. And now, at the King and Queen, I have one of my own. I'm at the bar right now, and I am being served by an American barmaid.

She's wiry, outgoing, obviously athletic, and very friendly. Too friendly. You can just tell she jogs. She probably has a scrapbook filled with photos of all of her friends on spring break, mixed in with cut-out pictures of sexy men in advertisements. 'LUV U 4-EVA' is spelled somewhere in purple felt-tip.

Mel, the pub manager, introduces Lisa to me, for obvious reasons – we're both Yanks. And then it starts. The networking. 'So, I'm doing ad campaigns for a charity and, like, I'm *totally* interested in getting you on board . . .'

I nod politely, but inside I'm crying. Here I am, in my pleasant sanctuary filled with old men, musky pets and stained carpets, and there's an intruder. The intruder being the relentless, go-getting American female, bent on making life better for everyone and saving the world. There she is, with her flat midriff, toned biceps and perfect teeth. Oh, those teeth again, so white and straight you could show a movie on them.

Why is this bothering me so much? I know it's not her fault. She's a sweet girl, and a delight to look at. But she's also the embodiment of America – an extremely competent and highly competitive enterprise. She scares me. For nearly two years, I've lulled myself into a declining state of incompetence. I prefer not to excel. I wish to enter no races unless it's to the toilet. And now, here is that spirit of enterprise once again, from America, invading my space of apathy.

I haven't heard an American female voice in a long time, and I forgot how relentless it sounds. American women talk loudly, in an over-friendly manner, usually about their Tonkinese short-haired cat. Every statement sounds like a question, a need for approval.

'So, I am like a psych major from Brown?' 'And can I tell you how much I hate George Bush?' 'And London is like so awesome?'

They pepper their sentences with useless words, including 'like', 'you know', 'amazing' and 'awesome'. British women do this too, but they only abuse one word, which is 'brilliant'. Worse than that: an American woman trying to act like a British one saying how 'brilliant' everything is. See 'Gwyneth Paltrow'. Then, you know, shoot her.

The boys sitting with me find the new barmaid irresistible, simply because she is different from the British ones they are used to.

'It's like she came from a shampoo commercial,' says Dave, his tongue slipping past his teeth. I try to tell him it's just novelty that's playing a trick on him. Because, you know, the same thing happens to me with British girls. But they won't buy it.

I've started to miss the old British barmaid from before, whatsherface. She was the ideal antidote to the American waiter or waitress. Unlike her US counterpart, she was not working on a screenplay, acting in an off-Broadway play about incest, or singing in an all-nude exposé on Watergate. She was just a barmaid, doing her barmaid job. No one could fetch a pint faster, and she was always there to empty an ashtray, using a paintbrush and an empty Clover butter container. She didn't bore you with stories about her career – you were watching her career right there. She also kept her mouth shut, which was good, if you'd ever seen her teeth.

60. BALD GUYS AND BEER BELLIES

I hate the mirror. I'm looking at myself, naked, and it's incredible (not in a good way). I am not only losing my hair but also my butt. It's an interesting thing about growing old – as your belly grows, your arse flattens. It makes no sense but I am glad it's happening here in the UK, and not in the US. In the UK, men know how to age and women accept it. They know what to fight and what not to fight, and they know they can't fight growing old. Most men here don't even bother. It's another rejection of competition that I can get behind.

At the pub across the road, a man sits there alone. He plays almost nothing on the jukebox but Culture Club. 'Karma Chameleon' will play three or four times in the span of an hour. It's a strangely focused enterprise on his part. He feeds the machine with pounds, then returns to a comfortable chair, and sits . . . and listens. He does not move until the songs are played out. And then he gets up and he repeats it. It's this single-minded dedication that, in others, wins Nobel Prizes.

I know a lot about this guy because I am there as much as he is. Well, with the possible exception of the Glass Gatherer, who is wiping up my table at the King's Arms. Just about every pub has one of these old fellas. He is usually in his early sixties, or maybe he could be thirty-five and just looks that old. The one I know has unkempt hair styled like candy floss, and he periodically gets up and walks around the pub, picks up empty glasses and returns to the bar. For his efforts he gets a free drink. I look at him now, and ask myself, just what am I looking at? Me, in five years.

I should be so lucky. I think it was George Bernard Shaw who said that youth is wasted on the young. Well, so is hair. I am closing in on forty-one and already losing some of my precious locks. I'm just another step closer to becoming a fat, balding Brit. Meanwhile, every man at work under twenty-eight has pointy hair, plastered by gels and creams. I am obsessed with this practice, and I admit that sometimes I wish I could do it myself. (I have tried to, but never on my head.)

Rhombus hair is everywhere. But only among the men in their twenties. When a British man hits a certain age, let's say twenty-eight, it starts to happen . . . he loses his hair and his face gets fat. I have noticed this in my office; every man over twenty-eight has a bald or freshly shaved head and puffy cheeks. Some of these men have grown goatees. It's like they've turned their heads upside down, with the pointy stuff on the bottom.

It's a cruel joke: young British men could be rock stars in America, for five years. Then, all of a sudden, their hairline shifts and the next day they're Kojak. But no one is attempting to preserve what they've got. Once the hair starts going, the men shave it off.

I admire this practice. In America, most men refuse to go bald. They wear baseball caps or hairpieces, get hairplugs, or smear regenerative goop into their scalps. An American friend called Bob went bald in his mid-twenties. For the past ten years he's experimented with toupees, rugs, weaves and hats. Thanks to good genes, he is very tall, so you can't really see how horrible his head looks from all his disastrous attempts at cranial camouflage. He is the perfect example of how not to go bald. Once a hairline recedes in England, though, the British seem to embrace it. It's this kind of thinking that helps explain why most Brits aren't that stressed. Imagine having to think about your hair all the time. Now, imagine not having to think about your hair all the time. That's got to be easier on your psyche. It sure beats rubbing Propecia into your scalp and then watching your pillow grow hair.

It's the same deal with being fat. You should see my belly now. I'm looking at it as I type. It's not hard to because the laptop is teetering on it. I look pregnant. Pregnant with ale. The average British male has a belly but that belly is different from the American one. When the American male gets fat, the weight expands sideways and also settles on the rear, resembling a pear on two legs. In the UK, the belly is slim at its sides. In fact, if you're standing behind a British male, you wouldn't know he has a belly because he has no flabby love handles. It's only when he turns and you see his profile that you see his pot. I attribute this to the fact that Yankee fat comes from the immense volume of food we shove down our swollen faces. We are served larger portions of great-tasting food, and we force ourselves to eat everything until we puke, like geese bred for foie gras. British fat is purely alcohol-derived. You drink everything in sight until, of course, you can't see. Coupled with the fact that most British food defies eating in mass quantity, and that creates an entirely different kind of belly.

I call it a Brit pot. And it's not pretty, but no one seems to care.

I don't. Back in the States, I fretted about my weight. I exercised every morning for two hours. I also ran after work, skipped meals and did crunches until my abs cried. I was obsessed with my body, intent on winning a war that was pointless to fight. Now I realize I was an idiot.

Brits also seem pretty content with having imperfect teeth. Americans spend a crap load on straightening their teeth. I had braces for three years and my sister wore an elaborate piece of metal headgear that wrapped around her jawline – not unusual for girls, for they all seemed imprisoned in scaffolding.

I bet you don't know what a retainer is, but I had to wear one for three years after I got my braces off. It's a device created by orthodontists to help hold teeth in their new position after your braces are removed. It's made from wire and plastic, and moulded to fit your mouth. It's usually red. I dropped mine many times during school and rarely cleaned it. Once it fell in the toilet. By the time I got rid of it, it smelled like the inside of a work boot.

Talk to any American, and they'll tell you how their most common nightmare is losing their teeth. It's inexplicable, much like a British man's need to wear black socks with shorts. In the UK, I suppose, there is an implicit understanding that straight teeth do not make you happy. So why straighten them? They add character! They can open beer bottles!

Maybe the state of your teeth reflects the British mind. Brits don't pay too much attention to their weathered enamel, and a slight to moderate state of disrepair is perfectly acceptable. I think Brits hold the same attitude about their houses, jobs, spouses, pop stars and government. You don't need perfect teeth and you certainly don't need perfect pop stars. That would be boring. Flaws are what make this country great. Flaws are the secret to enjoying good parts of an agreeable life.

But, back to me for a moment. My teeth are still pretty straight, but they've yellowed from all the smoking. My belly continues to swell, and my hair is retreating slowly. I am now almost completely pale. I am like one of those four-legged fish, called the Ichthyostega, the one that lived in Greenland 400 million years ago (give or take a million). Considered the missing link between fish and land animals, it could stiffen its body and walk on land with flippers. In a sense, like that fish, I'm going through my own physical evolution, from an American to a Brit. But without the flippers.

61. NEW YEAR'S EVE AT THE KING AND QUEEN

Elena and I are in our apartment, getting ready to go out. We have dinner plans, and really, that's about it. It's not that I hate New Year's Eve; it's that I hate people who love New Year's Eve. I love going out with friends and getting drunk, but I hate the pressure to go out with friends and get drunk. Anything that must be forced always ends up a failure, and around midnight you simply wish you were at home, in bed, watching reruns of *The Office* while eating chips. I hate New Year's Eve especially when it's in New York. Usually we end up at some club, one with bottle service, which runs to around three hundred bucks before you even tabulate the actual booze. During the evening, someone will slip you a line of coke, and then the rest of the evening you're spent chasing that someone for another. I think I did this four years in a row.

This New Year's Eve, it's going to be different. I am going to take Elena to a restaurant with my friend Dave and his girlfriend, and have a nice meal and a bottle of wine. There will be no hoopla. Or anything that might resemble hoopla. Nope. This is going to be boring.

We head to a barren French steakhouse – it's as empty as Keira Knightley's stomach. There we share a couple of bottles of wine and come up with a plan. It's New Year's Eve, after all. We MUST do something special. And so, we do. We go to the pub. The same pub I was at the previous night, and the night before that. The King and Queen.

When we get there, it's filled with the same crew of similar faces from around the neighbourhood, all wearing hats and blowing little horns and dancing to Duran Duran. The lights are dimmed – it's dark and cold in the pub but the sweat from a group of dancing fat ladies warms the place up like a campfire. We drink, dance and take some pictures, none of which are coming out in the darkness. We celebrate the New Year not with a bang, but a whimper, swigging bad rosé and smoking. And then we stumble home on an empty street.

It's incredibly quiet. I could have pooped in the middle the street and no one would have noticed. This is a nice way to spend a New Year's. Pooping in the middle of the street.

It beats an earlier one I spent in New York, when I got arrested. It was a few years ago, in Times Square. I ended up in handcuffs and driven to the Tombs, in downtown Manhattan. From the street, the jail only looks one storey tall, but this massive jail sinks deep into the ground. I got locked up because I was trying to have fun. I wasn't planning on going out, you see, but it was New Year's Eve, so I forced myself. And an hour later, I was sitting across from a guy pulling pubic hairs out of his crotch and placing them in his mouth, then removing them and sticking the hair ball to the back of his shoe. There was a rapist dozing next to me. Sorry, make that an 'alleged' rapist.

I spent that night with one eye open, peering through the sleeve of my rolled-up jacket. When I made it to court, I was placed next to another man, masturbating furiously. When he climaxed, it was against my thigh. In a few hours, I was released into the pouring rain.

I only tell you this story because a) it's a good story, and b) it's why I love New Year's Eve right now. New Year's Eve at the King and Queen is a shabby affair with cheap lights and dancing fatties but it sure beats Times Square, where the converging, craning mass of humanity desperate to be anywhere but home makes you want to eat your own face off.

Having said that, next New Year's Eve, I won't be at the King and Queen, I'm sure. I'll try something different. Maybe the King's Arms. They've got Culture Club on the jukebox and an amazing supply of Twiglets.

62. STRAIGHT HAIR AND BIG BELTS

It's January and it's freezing. I am wandering down Oxford Street, accidentally. I try to avoid the place because it's manically over-crowded, almost always with groups of teenage girls. They frighten me. Here comes a group now – they always travel in groups! – dressed in almost nothing, even though it's a winter evening and I'm shivering under a long coat. They're in short tops and little skirts. The only thing they wear of substance is big fat belts. Women in London love their big belts – they're all as wide as the M5.

Jenni tells me that when you see girls walking around in icy conditions without a coat, 'Don't be mistaken into thinking they are uneducated or broke. They are simply showing off their new designer top, from a factory outlet, of course.'

Worse, none of these girls are wearing any socks. They must have incredibly smelly feet!

They're all tanned too – fake, I presume – which is also why they're wearing so little clothing. If you're paying to look brown, you better make sure it's not wasted only on the mirror. Other people must see how golden brown you are, even if, by contrast, the tan makes your eyes pop out like a marmoset's.

But all is forgiven when I see their hair. All of these girls on Oxford Street look the same in that they have the straightest, most perfect hair I have ever seen. Sadly, one girl seems to have screwed with her perfect locks – tormenting them with a blonde fringe.

'Girls usually between fourteen and fifty-two who have blonde/yellow/orange fringes are basically all the people who are influenced by anyone from Pamela Anderson to Britney, and want to be blonde,' Jenni tells me. 'This is the closest they will ever get.'

I don't know why they bother. British women have perfect hair. It's shiny, flat – I can see myself in it! I don't see this kind of hair in America, and I have a theory: American girls have more options, and hairdressers are far cheaper. That means you see more variety among women's hair, not all of it very good. But British girls have one option and one option only: the hair straightener. And they've become so good at straightening their hair that it's become an art form. I like it. But I'm too scared to tell them because I think they might hit me.

63. THE PUB TOILET DOOR

I have been spending a lot less time at work and more time in the pub. Elena doesn't mind because it keeps me from smoking in the flat. I think this is what happens over time, to anyone who moves to London. I think it's called acclimatization, but it feels more like becoming a drunk. But also, my job has become less interesting than the pub. In fact, mostly everything is less interesting than the pub.

The pub never ceases to surprise me. For example: I am enthralled by the pub toilet and not in a George Michael kind of way. British toilets are called toilets, because they are TOILETS. Shitholes, to be precise. In America, we call them rest rooms – odd, since it's the last place in the world you'd want to rest, unless of course you're a turd.

I am in the toilet now, urinating against a flat sheet of metal. Whenever I do this wearing sandals, my toes get pleasantly sprinkled with back-splatter. It's disturbing and refreshing, in a morning-dew-in-the-country, lurid kind of way.

The best part of the toilet, however, is the cubicle graffiti. Usually it comes in threes: kicked off by a racist, added to by an anti-racist, then finished off by a satirical wag. This is known, at British universities, as the 'bog triplet'. Example:

Racist: BNP rules. Foreigners fuck off home!
Anti-racist: Don't be silly, you fucking racist plum
Twerp: My plums are purple!

It's that kind of writing that makes pissing on my foot worth it.

Here is a fun fact: the reason why the toilet is called the loo is because a British company made a toilet called 'Waterloo' in honour of the famous battle. Over time, it lost the first two syllables, flushed away without so much as a courtesy wipe. Brits call it a 'bog', and toilet paper is referred to as 'bog roll'. This is all new to me. We don't have bogs in America. England has lots of bogs, apparently, and you put them to good use. I've always wanted to enter the World Bog Snorkelling Championship, which appears every August Bank Holiday in a peat bog somewhere in mid-Wales. But I'm a terrible swimmer.

Back to toilets – nothing about the British kind makes sense to me, especially the fact that, unlike its US counterpart, I always leave a trail of poop in the bowl. My wife despises me for it. I don't understand why. I return to the table at the King's Arms, and ask my British friend Ross, who says, 'That's pre-war plumbing. You've got to remember that most of our grandparents can remember going into the garden for a shit. Bringing the toilet indoors was a big deal, and so was the amount of water you would comfortably allow sloshing around at the bottom of your new indoor toilet. By nature we are a cautious nation – too much water in the bog means a risk of flooding, plus you don't want to appear too flash when the neighbours come round for tea. Lack of water, with small piping, equals skid marks. The good news is that there's not a man in Britain who doesn't know how to unblock a toilet.'

I knew I wasn't crazy. Every time I poop, I have to use this horrible toilet scrubber – a disgusting appliance that, like Paris Hilton, gets dirtier with each use. I do miss the American toilet – wide, deep and expansive, like our Grand Canyon. But, you know, for your butt.

Ross takes a gulp and calls me on it.

'American toilets? Jesus, you could swim in them! I've managed to wash my nuts on at least three occasions in a Yank toilet, and have full sex in a urinal.'

That is the downside of American toilets, of course, and it's a big one. We call it 'splashback', a phenomenon unknown to Brits because your toilets are too shallow to cause it. It's when you poop and water splashes back up, decorating your testicles. I read somewhere (it might have been in *The Economist*) that it's a harmful health risk because splashback water contains *E. coli* bacteria. It's not so bad for the person on the bowl, but lethal for anyone who might give that person a blowjob in the hours afterward.

When I exit a pub toilet, I always find myself in front of another door, which I suppose is called 'the fire door', but I could be wrong. This is the best part of the pub toilet because it eliminates the possibility that someone might actually see you urinating. This is a common occurrence in American bathrooms when you have only one door separating the public from your exposed, floppy genitalia. On numerous occasions, while peeing, my eyes have met others while they walk past the rest room door as it's opened – an act that immediately freezes me up. (I have what's called 'gentleman's bladder', a condition that prevents me from peeing if other humans are around. I would have been a wreck in the army. It causes me to stand for long periods in public toilets, doing nothing. The upside is that I've met many British MPs that way.)

Despite my fears of urinating in public, I am now drunk enough to try an open-air urinal, and I am wandering through Soho, dying for a wee. I happen upon a strange, tall, boxed, street urinal. I decide to use it and realize that, as I unbutton my pants, everyone on the street knows what I am doing. My genitals are out, but all anyone can see is my back. I find it utterly ingenious that, if I were to pull out my penis on Wardour Street, I could be arrested for indecent exposure. But if I coax urine out on the very same street, I am perfectly fine. I can't be the only person that finds the idea of openly urinating in a town square to be both objectionable and stimulating.

I tell my mate Dave about this afterwards.

'I've never heard of this,' he says. 'You sure you weren't pissing in a phone booth?'

64. DARTS

I meet a few friends at Goodge Street, at a different pub this time because, for some reason, they've all taken up darts. It was a group decision, apparently, made without my knowledge. And that hurts my feelings.

I am sitting at a tall table flicking my ash and drinking a pint, watching three mates compete against a few other strangers. There's a strange board hanging on the wall, and numbers written in chalk. It's hard to believe this sport is nationally televised. But I think, hell, why not? It may be the most British phenomenon there is: the entire darts world is contained inside pubs. It rewards people who can concentrate and do mental arithmetic while drunk; it's horse-tranquillizingly repetitive; it's the precision hurling of nails into cork-board – basically, it's long-distance DIY.

'Everybody in Britain knows it's shit,' says Chris, 'yet everybody loves darts, probably for two reasons: 1) it's the only sport the rest of the world sees as pointless enough for Britain to be able to dominate; 2) there's a bar.'

I sit and watch because I am too afraid that I might hurt someone. I am terrible at any games requiring dexterity, which means all games. I suppose this is why darts is played in a pub. If you do get punctured, or worse, lose an eye, chances are you will be too drunk to feel it. I continue watching, gently lulled into a state of tranquillity. I know somewhere in the US there is a sports bar where a man is throwing basketballs into a basket. I bet he calls the bartender 'Chief', and knows all the words to 'Cherry Pie' by Warrant. Thank God I'm here.

65. MUSHY PEAS

I am at a chip shop, a few blocks from work, and I'm drunk again. I order a cheeseburger.

'What are you doing?' Jenni asks. 'Get a battered sausage.'

I change my order. The man behind the counter hands me a crusty fried tubular object. I immediately bite into it and, although the fried batter seems an appropriate temperature, the meat within sets my mouth on fire. I spit half of it out on to the pavement. I look over at Jenni, and she's shoving something green into her mouth.

'Mushy peas,' she says. 'Want some?'

I take a forkful, and it feels like baby food.

'That's a relief,' I say, as the weird paste collects in my stomach. 'What did I just eat, exactly?' I ask her.

'Dried peas that are boiled until they're a paste. They're great with butter.'

She is also eating a sandwich. A 'chip butty' – two slices of bread with 'chips' or French fries in them. I think to myself: this is the nation which, until relatively recently, ruled the world.

I suddenly realize why British food is so unique. It's only to be eaten when drunk, because it was designed for drunks. Most of these delicacies can be held in one hand, without need of utensils. And with mushy peas, one does not even require teeth to consume it. Given the nature of dentistry in England, this makes perfect sense. I could eat like this for ever.

66. HERPES

I am at the office now, hung over, and I've just exited a meeting that hasn't helped matters. Things aren't going well. Our circulation is down, and people are starting to worry that the magazine may be in trouble. The good news is that we've been offered an interview with a former British racing driver. I'm told he is a legend. One of my employees, Nick, fills me in: he has taken part in over 500 races, but was often known as 'the greatest driver never to win the World Championship'. That's got to be good.

Because he asked, I send Nick to do the interview. Nick asks him about the good old days when he was racing. The legend replies that he spent most of that period 'spreading herpes throughout the world'.

According to Nick anyway.

Shortly after the magazine comes out with that quote inside, the legend leaves three messages on my phone. All of them are very polite, genial even, but concerned.

'I never said I was spreading herpes,' he says. 'I remember saying I was spreading *happiness*. I'm afraid the writer got it wrong.'

I call him immediately. He's not there. I leave him a long message, apologizing profusely, knowing that it probably wouldn't help. But then he calls me back, chuckling.

'Just write a correction,' he tells me before calling the writer a 'stupid twat'. The next issue, I run an apology. No lawyers or settlements are involved. Eventually the problem went away. Unlike Nick, who I probably should have canned, the bastard.

This experience sums up why I love UK celebrities. Unlike their American counterparts, they're not up their own asses. If that had been an American star who we had accidentally besmirched, I'd be living in a cardboard box under an overpass.

I've met a few UK celebrities and although they may not be as attractive as the Yanks, they're amazingly low-key, without ego and approachable. They wear their mistakes proudly, and will even star in programmes aimed specifically at exposing their own foibles. Right now I'm watching a programme on Daniella Westbrook. Or rather, her nose. She has had it repaired a number of times, due to prolonged and monumental cocaine use. She has lost her septum, and she has no problem discussing it. She makes me smile.

British celebrities are far superior to Americans for that reason: they are simply messier. I can think of several who fit this description. One balding no-good plum who has done little but appear in celebrity reality TV shows has no shame in living off his dead dad's name. He even looks tired and bored with his own face. There's a feted young actor who screwed his kid's nanny, and still manages to smirk like a chimp in a soiled nappy. Then there's a *Daily Sport* model I met at one of my parties. I watched her deck a bartender and get hauled off to jail. She just got arrested again this morning, as I write, for punching out a window in Prophecy nightclub. She needs her own show.

I adore Kerry Katona – a pumpkin-headed moppet who always seems to be in a crisis. I am repulsed by and obsessed with Pete Doherty, that Moss-shagging addict with amazing taste in hats and women. He's one of the few people in contemporary society who might have the plague. I see Ricky Gervais weekly, walking down the street wearing a really lousy racing jacket. It makes him look ridiculous, but he doesn't mind. And then there's Karl Pilkington. He lives around the corner from me, and I run into him daily. He thinks I'm stalking him, but I'm not. We just happen to share the same neighbourhood. Anyway, he won't answer any of my letters, including the one requesting his toenail clippings.

In the UK, British celebrities feel they are 'celebrated' in a nation slowly declining. US celebrities, though, generally assume they are 'worldwide' celebrities, so they tend to believe in their own publicity. And this is why, for the most part, they should be killed.

67. THE PUB QUIZ

Dave, my skinny, large-headed 'mate' has left me a message about a pub quiz at a bar called the Washington in Belsize Park. I've seen signs in front of pubs all over London, but I've never been to one myself, mostly out of fear.

'Quizzes . . . you pay a pound each, someone asks a load of questions about anything,' Dave says. 'Winner gets a load of booze, though of course you're already drunk by then.'

I imagine that's the reason for so many quizzes at every pub. Landlords do it knowing that once you enter a quiz you can't leave. All there is to do is drink, and you now have captive drinking and spending audience.

I'm pretty good at trivia, and I love to drink, so it only makes sense that I attend. I throw on some trousers and head to the tube on Goodge.

We're at the bar, and already drunk. A man makes an announcement that the quiz is about to begin, and we're asked to ante up a pound or so to play. I look around the pub and notice it's packed – each table manned by a team that seems to be taking this exercise as seriously as a roadside drug test.

The first couple of questions have to do with obscure British entertainers, and Dave manages to get them right. Lucky for us, there are a few questions regarding American history, which allows me to flex a little Yankee muscle. Of course, I miss the question on which state Mt Rushmore resides in. I blame that on the Stella, although it's more likely the fact that I slept through most of my history classes.

When the winners are announced, we are delighted to find out that we've come in fifth place. First through third place get prizes, which range from a bottle of wine, to two bottles of wine. But then something goes haywire. A shouting match erupts between two teams. The fourth place team has accused the third place team of cheating. The accused, a group of slender admin types in stripy polo shirts, try to defend themselves by laughing dismissively, then slinking away into a dark corner. But to no avail. It becomes clear they are guilty.

'Those fucks were using their phone to get answers via text,' Dave tells me. 'It always happens. But it's criminal.' The men get kicked out, and everyone cheers.

And now it's back to straight drinking. We're drunk, but we're also, for some reason, straining for conversation. Which is pretty depressing, after the excitement of the quiz. It is then I realize that the quiz is wonderful because it means we don't have to talk to each other, but can still be in the pub. Now that we are stuck talking to each other, I realize how important not talking to each other is. It's also an easy method of proving our knowledge and/or superiority, even though both often don't exist. And it's done without hurting anyone in the process. It sure beats arm wrestling, or riding a mechanical bull.

68. EARL GREY IN A CHIPPED MUG

No matter what happens in British life, you can count on one thing: someone offering you a cup of tea. Tea is the beginning and ending for everything. You sit down with someone, you have tea. You kick them out of your flat, you have tea. You get ready for work, you make tea. You come home and have tea. When you are not making tea, you are probably thinking about making tea. The world is a teapot, frankly, and we're just living in it.

In fact, when God made the earth, you just know he couldn't have done it without Earl Grey. Tea is life's punctuation. It may be background noise to a Brit, but it means a lot to me, because it undermines any effort to rush out and do anything. You can't simultaneously make tea and do anything productive. That's impossible. Having tea means stopping, slowing down, and looking out of a rain-spattered window. It's the pause button that simply doesn't exist in America.

Everywhere I go, people offer me tea. And it makes everything better.

For example, my boss just offered me tea. And now he's telling me the company won't renew my contract. I came in this morning for my job review and I knew it wasn't going to be good. The numbers are bad, and when the numbers are bad, somebody has to take the fall. Still, the boss was nice enough to offer me tea first.

I suppose if I were back in Manhattan, I would be feeling pretty awful. The last time I got fired was in New York, and I didn't take it well. But back then I never drank tea. Here I drink it constantly. I don't know this for a fact, but I am assuming that's why, now I'm being fired, it really doesn't matter. My boss returns with my tea – milky, sugary and weak – made by Jenni, who makes tea better than anyone else on the planet . . . because it's milky, sugary and weak. This is great tea, even in a chipped mug.

'I'm afraid we won't be renewing your contract,' Bruce tells me, as I sip. Fine, I think. I am staring out of the window, it's raining, and the tea is fantastic.

I skip out that afternoon, and meet my ex-workmates at the pub. We all get a little drunk. But not a lot. I know I will miss all of them, but I live just around the corner. There has been no commiserating or sadness, or late-night calls to drug dealers. I know it's time to go, so I suppose this is what you'd call 'growth'. I don't know. Buzzed and excited, I am living in London and now unemployed. Just like many other people living in London, I suppose. At least I still have my teeth.

And now, at home in my underwear, I make tea. Tea is the ultimate symbol of what's great about England: that no matter how crappy life can be, it's really not so bad if you've got a decent cup of tea. But I could use some toast.

69. SAINSBURY'S BACHELOR ALLEY

I have no fresh bread. Bread here goes mouldy faster than my unwashed underpants. That means I'm off to the local Sainsbury's, the most beguiling store on earth.

It's around the corner and, in a jog, I am there. I nod to the security guard, whose eyes are always a deep bloodshot red. He mumbles something to me. He appears as high as a kite. He smiles. I can't tell if he likes me or if he thinks I am a giant bird.

It's lunchtime for those who work, and I am lost among a mass of suits and dresses in front of the wall stuffed with sandwiches. It's a vibrant, noisy place and I stand out in my track bottoms and button-down shirt. I recognize people from the old sales team at work and, studying my wardrobe, they wisely avoid my gaze. I am flanked by a number of striking women in skirts, all wearing those massive belts. And they love their phones too. Their ears are glued to their mobiles as they read sandwich availability back to the bosses at headquarters. 'Egg and cress . . . no, egg AND cress. Tuna and sweetcorn. Yes, tuna AND sweetcorn! They're out of red salmon and cucumber. No. No. Cheddar and celery? One left! I'm going to get the roast chicken salad!' I imagine this is what the stock market is like. But with sandwiches.

I enjoy going there as an unemployed sap in my sweatpants because it reminds me that there is life outside my flat, and it keeps me from losing myself in the live feed of *Big Brother*. Here I find real human life in all its glory, fighting over sandwiches. The women are intense. There's nothing busier or more important than a British woman on her lunch break.

I make two trips to Sainsbury's every day. My second trip occurs around 7 p.m. I go usually to buy a tub of cold pasta, which is the only ready-made food left. The atmosphere at the store is empty and grim. The wall of sandwiches is now barren, and all you find are these lonely tubs of wilted penne pasta. It becomes a chilly reminder of what you will look forward to if you don't find a good woman to settle down with. Which is a tub of cold carbohydrate. The only people buying them are bachelors. I see them, staring blankly at the nearly empty trays. They stoop to pick up something at the back – a bowl of reddish lentils with chicken, maybe. They stare at it closely, almost willing it to change into something they'll actually love.

I don't know why I go there, and I don't know why anyone goes to 'the wall of doom' at this time of the evening. It's not for the sake of their finances. The men I see there dress well. I wonder if it's simply ambivalence that drives people there. You don't care what you eat, you just know you're supposed to eat. Which leads me to . . . Rustler Burgers.

I love Rustler Burgers. But they hate me. Microwave them for 70 seconds, and they're as limp as a whale's penis. I find out later that if I turn the burger over and let it stand for a minute, it cooks through and hardens up. It's this little tip that makes evening meals so memorable. I am assuming the Rustler Burger is a British invention and, if it is, then I love the British take on American food. Which is not very good. Actually, it's awful.

I buy Rustlers often, like tonight. I buy them even though trying to open their packaging is almost as harrowing as eating the food inside it. Generally, it takes me a good fifteen minutes of pulling at the edges of the packaging before I give up and start stabbing at the cellophane with a knife. Also the only time I buy Rustlers is when I'm drunk so it could take hours. I wonder how many people have died trying to open a Rustler burger. Probably more than those who tried to eat one.

Rustlers underline my belief that American food doesn't have to be great to be good. It doesn't even have to be good to be good. It can actually be pretty horrible, and it's still, you know, not half bad. So I buy Rustlers in part to remind myself how simple US cuisine is, and also because I'm just really, really drunk.

I have just bought six Rustlers convinced I would eat three 'now' and three 'later'. I have eaten one, I feel ill, and now I've thrown them all away. I wouldn't have this problem if Sainsbury's stocked alternatives. It is the least practical and strangest store on the planet, because it's a 'local', and they do not believe in stocking products that people actually need or want. This is the only store I know that runs out of shopping bags. They do have eggs though, which they keep unrefrigerated. In America, eggs are kept in the constantly chilled dairy section, where they belong. In the UK, they are kept next to non-perishable items like cereal and butt lotion. It makes no sense to me, but I'm not complaining. I am just happy they have eggs to begin with. It beats eating their steak.

Which I have just purchased on my third trip back to the store. I always buy steak, but it always comes out chewy and stale, like an eight-ounce fillet of corrugated board, the kind that resists crushing under compression. I slice into my latest attempt, and it's no better, not even with a coating of mayonnaise – a Russian trick designed to con people into thinking they're actually eating food. It still doesn't work. Fuck it. I'm going across the street to the sushi place, Soho Japan. Above the restaurant, however, is the best thing on the menu. It's the fat man who hangs in front of the second-floor window, shirtless.

70. THE FAT MAN ACROSS THE STREET

If I look out my window every morning around 10 a.m., I can see him. He leans shirtless out of his window, his belly hanging over the ledge like a sack of mail no one in their right mind would want delivered. He stares out of that window every day, the same perturbed expression pasted across the front part of his head, as if to say about the present state of affairs that he could have done better. I stare at him, and sometimes he stares back at me. We've been doing this for months now. And I, shirtless and bulging, realize that perhaps he is as close as I get to a mirror of myself in about thirty – no, ten years.

For now though, he makes me feel skinny. You know what else makes me feel skinny? Large shirts, which I buy because the other ones don't fit any more. I just bought a pair of size 36 pants. Size 36! That's the waist. My inside leg is 29. I am now wider than I am long. Along with this weight gain, other weird things are happening to me, or more specifically, my body.

I tried running yesterday, and my shorts bunched up between my porcine thighs. And stayed there. I probably should start wearing a tennis skirt or something that reduces the chafing. The sweating and rubbing that comes from running makes any form of exercise a painful practice, like awakening an army of slumbering fire ants between my legs. Oddly, perhaps as a consequence, I am growing things on my body. I have discovered a bit of skin hanging from my inner thigh. The following day, it has a partner – both are smooth morsels of flesh, the size of a barley grain, but slightly darker.

This whole experience has left me sad, confused and, according to a medical dictionary, 'peduncled'. A 'peduncle' is the stalk the skin tag hangs from, although it sounds vaguely perverted, like the guy married to your aunt who's more interested in your young cousins. Meanwhile, I've grown what's called a 'fat pad', or an adipose apron. It's roughly the size of a waist smock that B&Q employees wear, but it's made of fat. Sadly, its effect on the genitals is not pleasant. It's a shame that as I get fatter, my penis doesn't grow too. But if it did, I guess there wouldn't be a man weighing under 24 stone.

Weight gain produces too many consequences to go into here, from one's gas now registering a 'G Basso' (up a minor seventh, a note apparently popularized in works by Verdi, who enjoyed his rigatoni, I'm told), to a constant battle against odour and sweat. It's enough to make me wear a kaftan: maybe something soft, light and smooth – a Korean koshibo accented with designed embroidery that adds a subtle touch of sophistication. Is that why Muslims wear burkhas? Is it not actually women in there, but instead their old magazine editors?

So I am now officially fat and smelly, just like the old man across the street, who's staring at me right now. I'm off to the gym, then. I need to 'lose a stone', or that's what the doctor has told me. A stone, I think, is somewhere between ten and fifteen pounds. It doesn't sound that bad. I just joined Fitness Exchange, hidden off the main drag of Tottenham Court Road. Inside, there's a pool, lots of machines, and a bunch of pleasant if sometimes irritating foreign fitness trainers who flex their delts even when they're taking a nap. There's not a British person at the front desk. There are some free magazines, though: mostly devoted to the joys of 'RV travel'.

In the locker room there's a man posing naked, inspecting every shred of cleaved muscle, every bulging tendon popping out between his hopeless, circa-1994 barbed-wire tattoos. It's so unnerving that I put away my camera phone. I realize then that I used to be this guy in the mirror. Consumed by my own image, I used to inspect every rope of muscle, convinced that unless I devoted hours a day to honing the mass, it all would decline into mush. What a horrible, horrible way to live.

I am now nothing like the guy in the mirror; I'm more like the guy leaning from the window. I suppose this is a big metaphor: instead of looking at myself, I'm now looking around, from the mirror to the window, meaning that how I look is far less important than what I'm looking at. I attribute this mainly to England, because there's so much to look at: the architecture, the girls and, of course, the clouds.

I've stopped weighing myself, by the way. I used to do it constantly. I needed to know, I suppose, like most Americans, how much I weighed at all times. I was always in constant competition, not with anyone but myself – or rather who I was a few weeks ago when I was fitter. I probably looked great on the outside but I felt like crap on the inside. Life is all about enjoying what's available to you, and you can't enjoy this planet if you're consumed by consumption.

I wonder if Brits have any idea how much they weigh. I don't think it matters much, or else you would have chosen a far more reliable marker than something called a stone. Plus, I rarely see any ginormously fat Brits, perhaps because they walk everywhere and the food just isn't good enough to gorge on. In America, food is plentiful and adorable – a burger from Jack in the Box practically begs you to fuck it. Food in England requires a commitment from you to accept its blandness. Taste is left to your imagination.

So now I'm fatter, slower and sweatier, surrounded by Brits who look pretty much the same way. I think, in England, men come to the gym not to build great bodies, but to allow themselves the right to get drunk afterwards. It's like putting money in the bank, so you can withdraw it later. And then, of course, vomit somewhere on Oxford Street.

Maybe in America, it's the pursuit of happiness that infects everything with competition. You can't go to the gym unless you match the efforts of everyone else. It's a good thing – it's why we have such great-looking aerobic instructors, cheerleaders and serial killers. But Christ, it's boring.

I prefer to avoid that and live large. To me, that's a far healthier mentality than my old life in NYC, where the pursuit of fitness only made the pursuit longer and more arduous. The harder I worked out, the harder I had to work out. In London, I think I've found out where I want to be, and it's the pub and not the gym. The only thing I'll be lifting there is a pint. I better put one in each hand to get a balanced workout.

71. GARDENING LEAVE

That's what it's called when you're fired. They put you on 'gardening leave'. I've been on it two months, the remaining part of my contract. In magazine publishing, 'gardening leave' is a strange term used instead of 'we're letting you go'. I love the phrase, because it sounds so bucolic. I imagine myself planting daisies and begonias, while wearing a silly hat and overalls.

Also: clogs.

I don't own clogs, but I still like the idea of gardening leave. It's a face-saving thing, not for the person fired but the person doing the firing. It's a perfectly British thing: instead of saying you're fired, the boss can say, 'Can you please leave, and we'll give you some money and please don't return with a hatchet and cut me to pieces.' And that's how it turned out. I don't own a hatchet.

Despite the name, gardening leave is far less active. It really means, 'sitting around the house, indulging a hobby, getting to know your kids'. The snag in all of this is that I don't have a house, I have no hobbies and I don't have any kids. So as an unemployed and pretty much unemployable man, I've done what one can only do: sleep in and then head to the pub. No matter how industrious I try to be, I usually end up in the pub by four. I've come to realize that if there's any city to be unemployed in, it's London.

My going-away party is tonight. It's in a pub a few streets away. It's not my normal hangout, which leads me to believe it was probably the cheapest and the only one my old colleagues could afford. They rented a small dank room upstairs, and outfitted it with Canadian flags and pictures of Canadian celebrities. (I should remind readers that I'm not Canadian.) I am told that Eoin, the managing editor who planned the party, had collected 'a few hundred quid' to throw the party. He spent all the cash on Canadian flags and pictures of Canadian celebrities.

Elena and I show up and, minus a few people, the entire staff is there. A cloud of awkwardness pervades: it's always weird to be the odd man out. You were once the boss, but now your colleagues no longer have to see you that way. They stare at you. I suppose the way one might stare at a ghost of a dead aunt in a dream. Unlike her though, I'm not naked.

But the weirdness dissipates once someone commandeers a manager's credit card and loads it up with tequila shots. After an hour or so, it feels like time to go, so Elena and I stumble down the stairs. Outside, while waving goodbye, I run into a tree. Somehow trees know when I drink.

It's morning now, and my head hurts. I've got no job. I've got nowhere to go and nothing to do. It's perfect. For now, I will wander and possibly drink somewhere nearby till my head clears. Once a boss, and now not a boss – I guess this is what it feels like to be English. No longer in power, you can pretty much do what you want. There is no pressure to perform, and you're out of the spotlight. Perhaps, I wonder, this is also what the after-life is like. Being dead means no pressure. Being dead means you can finally have fun! Being dead means the race is over. Being dead means being British. And if being dead means being British, then theoretically England is Heaven!

I must have hit my head on a tree.

72. GUM WADS ON KATE MOSS'S FACE

I've got an interview with an editor for a music magazine, in the hope of doing some freelance work. Normally, I'd take a cab, but extravagances like that are the first to go when you're broke. I'm taking the tube. I'm heading down the escalator of the station, which is my favourite part of the trip, by far. The escalators are steeper than any mountain, and sometimes it makes me dizzy. But that's not what makes the ride so delightful. It's the posters of models on the wall that accompany the journey – always scarred with strategically placed wads of bubble gum.

Here's what amazes me. Every single mug is marred with gum, but I've never seen anyone actually put the gum there. And I'm always on the lookout. I need to know who's doing it. I'd like to think it's a group of adorable schoolgirls, but I'd be happy too if it was the handiwork of a disgruntled special constable. Or perhaps a mobile disco DJ. My other primary suspects include: sinister priests, recently mugged pensioners, a pathetic wannabe TV presenter or a teenager working at McDonald's who has only a single star on his badge.

I hate the subway in New York City – perhaps because it scares me. It's dirty, alien and cold. It's much bigger and mostly confusing. I have only taken the Manhattan subway a few times, and each time I missed my stop, suffering anxiety attacks every time. Somehow, though, this never happens in London, even when I get lost or miss a stop. Instead, I've developed a pretty special relationship with this mode of transport – a love/hate thing not unlike a tumultuous marriage where one wonderful moment is followed immediately by something horrific.

The tube is like a brain puzzle in a newspaper – it always challenges me to think faster than I am used to. When I board a train I am asked to think as fast as the train, because I am never certain exactly where I am going. It's not that I don't read a map beforehand; it's just that, with the tube, destinations seem to change arbitrarily. And this affects your brain.

As the train moves, I stumble to a seat, and am quickly told by the voice of the conductor that my intended stop is being skipped. I read the subway map, moving up extremely close to the sign, agitating the begging Romanian beneath the colourful diagram. As I try to figure out where to transfer or where to get off I feel as though I'm trying to solve a difficult maths problem – and one that, if I get wrong, means I might end up without my pants in Harlesden.

It's this kind of suspense that makes travel fun. More importantly, it makes me feel good when I realize that as the train stops, this is the stop I actually need. It's like winning a lottery. Or maybe a balloon.

I quickly figure out that I've got to get off at the next stop and then transfer to another train, and then two more stops on that line will get me to my destination. Yes – I have achieved something grand!

It's pathetic that a grown man feels like he's cured cancer when all he's done is found an alternative route to an office in Islington. But so what! Every day I use the tube is another day that I feel like I'm something more than a gum wad of stupidity. The tube, for me, is an allegory for life. If you make a mistake, or an obstacle is thrown your way, there is always a way to fix it, or a way around it. And somehow, you'll always end up where you were intending to go. This is profound. I believe it is from a Leo Sayer lyric.

When I get on the tube, the trip never goes as planned. If I hop on the Northern Line, expecting to get to Camden from Goodge Street, I will always find the Goodge Street station closed. I will then walk to another station, and get on a train that will get me to King's Cross, where I can transfer. However, that day, the train isn't stopping at King's Cross, and there I go, passing the station by. But there's always another option – another way out – a solution for each problem presented.

I'm sitting on the tube, looking at everyone around me. No one talks, no one stares. They just read. Even the children read here, which is new to me. Here, no one bothers anyone – unlike New York City, where you might get pressed against a crazy person stinking of faeces.

I just missed the announcement! I love the announcements, and for the usual reasons. I like the accent, and I enjoy the choice of language. 'Please alight here for the British Museum'. I have never heard the word 'alight', but it sounds like something you would do in a hot air balloon.

I am staring at the tube map on the wall of the train, and marvelling at its simplicity. It wasn't until recently that I realized, though, that this arbitrary grid does not actually match the real layout of the city. I used to think that when I looked at the colourful red Central Line connecting Tottenham Court Road to Shepherd's Bush, I could simply walk down Tottenham Court Road, take a right, and walk straight to Shepherd's Bush. But I tried once and I found it impossible. I ended up making a series of detours, and ended up in Fulham. The tube map is like a coffin – useless until you're underground.

Using the tube as my only mode of transport does not help me truly understand the city. For that you need the bus. I am on one right now, and there's a gang of schoolgirls singing R&B songs at intimidating levels. They frighten me in a way that a gang of anything frightens you. It's as though they might meld together and beat me to death with monstrous schoolgirl fists. For some reason, just thinking about it arouses me. I should probably visit a doctor or something. Or at least learn some Craig David.

73. THE FOXTONS MINI COOPER

A close second to the bus, however, is a Mini Cooper driven by a Foxtons estate agent. The car is a horrible splash of puke-green paint mixed with yellow bolts of writing. If you look closely, you'll see that someone keyed the car all over the place. But if you look even closer you'll see that the vandalism is actually done on purpose – it spells out Foxtons!

I am in one of their garish little green cars now, sitting on the left-hand side (always a strange feeling), as a skinny young man with pointy hair, pointy shoes, and a pointy suit steers the golf-cart through the narrow streets of Notting Hill. Our lease is coming up, and Elena and I are looking for a place to live. And judging by the sheer number of Foxtons cars seen prowling the streets at any given time of day, they seem to be the only game in town.

Elena and I have been with Miles, the estate agent, on a number of trips, hitting four or five immensely overpriced apart-ments each day. No matter what price we give this ambitious young man, he shows us a flat so far out of our range that we get nosebleeds just hearing the price. When we tell him we can't afford it, he asks us if we can borrow from our parents.

I can't stand Miles, but I like his driving. And I've found that whenever I want to learn about a particular neighbourhood, the best thing to do is call Foxtons and tell them my wife and I are looking to buy a flat. An expensive one, at that! In minutes, they select four or five flats out of our price range and enlist the typical Foxtons estate agent to drive us around the area.

Every Foxtons agent looks the same. A mix of tailored clothing and hair gel, with more than a hint of Lynx, they seem to assess you only in pound signs. They smell of ambition and operate on insecurity.

While Miles drives, I ask him the same kinds of questions I might ask a tour guide. 'How old is that building there?' 'Who's the statue of?' 'Where's Buckingham Palace?' It's better than the Open Top from the Big Bus Company. It's much cheaper (free, actually), incredibly convenient and afterwards I always try to get him to drop us off at a pub.

Despite enduring Miles's commentary (always a passionate argument for buying now, rather than later), we get a thorough tour of the area, getting to know landmarks and often the names of his ex-girlfriends. I don't mind wasting his time, because I've realized that, with their jagged hairstyles and relentless pitch, all Foxtons agents are spawns of Satan.

'To be honest,' begins Miles, 'you aren't going to find the flat you want in your price range.'

Miles begins every other sentence with 'To be honest', suggesting that the remaining ones are lies.

So Elena and I decide that, no matter what, we won't buy a flat from Miles, but instead we'll use him to drive us around town. Over time we grow to enjoy his babbling, and I soon realize why: a Foxtons estate agent is the closest creature in the UK to the typical twenty-five-year-old ad executive living in Manhattan. Perhaps that's why I get off on their company – having them around reminds me how much I hated midtown sports bars and guys in suits who did coke off their mailbox keys. Foxtons agents are the least British people we know, so I guess it makes us enjoy the other Brits even more. Or maybe I'm just getting high off the fumes from the hair gel.

74. ASBOS

Here I am again, standing in front of the mirror, wondering who this new guy is. Every time I see my reflection, there always seems to be more of me staring back, and it's enough to drive me to drink. Which I do. And when I do drink, I make really dumb decisions – the kind that get me into trouble, prison or oversized Arsenal shorts.

See, it's Thursday night on a cool evening and I have agreed to play football against some kids. To be more precise: 'troubled' or 'problem' kids. That makes me nervous. Generally I dislike children, and when they become teens, that dislike turns to fear.

'Come on, Greg, they're twelve or thirteen,' Dave told me over a pint at the King's Arms. 'It'll be fun!' After four pints, I finally agreed and now I'm fucked. In England, dumb things are always agreed upon on the fourth pint. This is known as the 'rule of four'. I'm told it's how the War of the Roses and the Moody Blues got started.

And now, I am standing on the pitch at Coram's Fields, looking at these 'kids'. These are not your ordinary, runny-nosed, shove-your-postman kids. These kids are all taller than me, and they look like they kill postmen. I am scared shitless. Seriously, I have crapped so many times I am out of shit. This always happens to me when I get really nervous – I become a pneumatic frosting applicator on two legs, dispensing black fizz like an experienced cake decorator.

And now, dressed in my red, white and blue New England Revolution soccer jersey, which I borrowed, of course, I look even shittier. Much like me, the shirt is ugly, loud and American but, in the tradition of British fashion, I still wear black work socks (despite being unemployed). You'd never see that in America: we change our socks for every occasion.

The borrowed Arsenal shorts I am wearing are commemorative, bought during their final year at Highbury. I think I might commemorate them with more shit.

These kids I am about to play against are in fact teenage boys (aged thirteen to nineteen years) who, according to their coach Nadeem, were 'at risk for anti-social behavioural orders'. The acronym is ASBO, which is given to people who disrupt normal life – bullies, local drunks and eccentric pensioners who shout at hedges. If you get one, you are probably a bastard, and you will be banned from hanging out in places where bastards like you would normally hang out. I suppose that means shopping malls, chip shops and Grimsby.

Before the game, I read up on ASBOs. Indeed, these orders are designed to protect law-abiding citizens. But from what I can tell, kids take it as a badge of honour when they get one. And I don't blame them – every night there's a TV show portraying ASBO earners as modern-day pirates. And it's cool to scare the hell out of people. Especially, old people like me.

One thing I don't get: the way Britain seems to have withdrawn from disciplining its youth. In a way, sometimes I feel like England is a bit like the Old West, except instead of packs of wild Indians, you have gangs of sullen, acne-covered yobs in sportswear.

I read that if you breach an ASBO, you can go to jail or get fined. But if you're lucky a good guy like Nadeem will get you into 'structured football'. I am grateful for that, until I see them in front of me. There, on the field, I spy the 'kids' kicking a ball around. Most are taller than I had imagined, and they seem wholly unimpressed by me. They prove this by kicking a ball at my head. I duck as it whizzes by. Seconds later, another one comes barrelling at me. And then another. I decide to move as far away from the ball as possible. I'm now standing on a footpath in front of the changing rooms. I can't believe I'm doing this.

According to Nads (short for Nadeem, to his misfortune), the team has talent: players have contracts at clubs including Crystal Palace and Arsenal, with a few sure to go pro, 'when their testicles finally drop'. Armed with this new info, I am now terrified. Not only are they criminals, they are actually athletes.

Moments before the game starts, we take our positions. I am offered right defender, a position I played in youth soccer about thirty years ago. The whistle blows and people start moving. They are moving fast – much faster, in fact, than I'm used to. My eyes can't follow the action. But here comes an opposing player who has the ball and is dribbling towards me. He's not very tall. I can take him. Almost by instinct – a sense that had not been tapped in decades – I move in to make a sliding tackle. I miss him completely and, before I have time to see where he went, he's already scored, drunk water, bought a magazine and built a bong out of driftwood.

I soon realize that my body is no longer the body that lives in my head. Instead it's an older, slower, saggier body. It cannot deliver what my mind expects and, for the rest of the game, this realization is cruelly played out again and again. During play the ball seems attainable, but by the time I get to it, it's gone. Opposing players breeze past me without consciously noticing I'm there. To them I am just dog poop on the ground – something to be faintly aware of, but no threat. I take myself out four minutes into the first half and rest by curling vertically into a ball, palms on knees. From behind the goal I watch the kids score three more times.

It's now the second half, and the score is nearing double digits (although my side hasn't scored once), and I put myself back in. I am now playing 'right wing' and going up against defenders who frighten me. I am sweating copiously and there's a tingling in my arms. I am freaking myself out. Is that a bright light I see? Do not walk towards it. That's how people on soap operas die.

Terrified beyond comprehension, I am now in the centre of the action. Players on both teams are running all over the place so I decide to do the only thing that makes sense: stand still. It may be only a game, but I am lost in a machine featuring twenty working parts, and I don't want to get my arms or legs shorn off. After they score again, I remove myself from the field and return to the side-lines and collapse.

In the remaining minutes of the game, their best player, a tall cocky kid with dreads, takes a call from the sidelines. A buddy throws him a mobile and the guy continues playing while on the phone. He heads the ball.

We lose 9–2.

Before this game I had assumed that, when compared with American football, soccer (or your football) was as manly as Pete Burns. I ridiculed the game because it's easy: there's never any scoring, there's very little violence (except in the stands) and, more importantly, where are the cheerleaders? Without two teams of buxom girls in short skirts waving round balls of confetti this sport appears nothing more than a conspiracy to unite seventy thousand fat, balding blokes under one roof to hug.

But I was wrong. If I were playing American football I could probably fake it reasonably well, playing on defence, and resting on offence. What's great about that game is you really only play half of it, and even most of that time is spent in a relaxing huddle. That's why you see so many fat NFL players. You can be fat. But the athletes I saw today, they never rested. They were inhuman and they were beautiful. I hate them. You can't be out of shape when you play the beautiful game. You can't even be in good shape to play it. You have to be in great shape, and it probably helps if you're a criminal too.

After the game, waddling home to avoid the irritating experience of chafing thighs, I vow to lose weight. But first I needed to get something to eat. Maybe something healthy, for a change. Thank God for KFC.

75. CHICKEN FRIED CHICKEN

I can never find a KFC when I need one, but I can always find something that looks somewhat like it. Right now, I'm in line at Chicken Fried Chicken – at least, that's what I think the name is. It could also be Kentucky Cooked Chicken, Chicken Kentucky Fried House, Kentucky Fried Kentucky Chicken, Chicago Fried Kentucky Chicken House. All of them have a couple of things in common: their signs are red, and they sell chicken. Some of it is good, some of it awful. But I love them anyway.

The one I'm in now is small and dirty with white tiled walls. You can get chicken, fish, chips and some other stuff that appears to be food. I get three pieces of chicken, and sit on the pavement to eat it.

You don't find rip-offs of popular fast-food places in America. I guess these joints are proof of the capitalistic spirit that thrives heartily among recently arrived immigrants. They run dodgy and dangerous chicken/kebab shops – little joints that present the confused American many deep-fried options, all of them capable of creating life-threatening diarrhoea at affordable prices. In America, if you opened a Kentucky Chicken Fried Chicago Chicken shop, with a red and white bucket painted on the sign, you would be sued out of existence. You would lose your house, your car, and probably four of your fingers. Those fingers would be deep fried, extra crispy style, and served with corn.

76. ICE CUBES

But at least some of these chicken joints have ice cubes, which is more than I can say about the real KFCs in London. I am now in one on Goodge Street, and the delightful Polish woman on the counter won't give me any ice. But then, again, she never does.

In fact, I find that wherever I go ice is treated like bullion, to be hoarded or parcelled out in small pieces. What is the penchant for cafes and restaurants across this great country of yours to withhold ice from consumers? A soft drink, such as a Coke, always arrives without ice. When I ask for more ice, I am given two tiny cubes, along with a pained stare, as though I am pleading for a human kidney. Their human kidney. 'What do you need ice for?' says my friend Nick. 'Everything is supposed to be luke-warm or it's not British!' I've asked a lot of Brits why ice is so scarce, but no one has an answer. They do have theories:

- ice-making machines are relatively new and therefore cafes don't want them because they're too expensive. However, they still have to run their freezers to keep everything cold. This does not explain why, whenever you enter any newsagent, the Kinder Egg shells have already melted.
- it's never really hot in London, so who needs ice? Answer: I do. This is also a common explanation for lack of air con-ditioning – an explanation that doesn't help any of the thousands of old people who died in France back in 2003 because it was too damn hot that summer, and the doctors were away buying cheap sunglasses in Miami.
- Europeans like things to taste 'warmer' because it's natural. And some even believe that cold fluids can make you sick.

I think the real explanation, though, is closer to the idea of getting what you pay for. It simply makes more sense to skip the ice, since you're paying for the beverage. Ice is a rip-off – some-thing that Brits, especially those who remember the war, find reprehensible. 'When I go to a restaurant in the US, I always ask for no ice. That way I get what I pay for,' says Dave. 'Your tables at restaurants are also really thick. Did you ever notice that?' Yes, I tell him and leave to go to the toilet. He is consumed by the thickness of things in America. Which, I suppose, is why he hangs around with me.

77. SWANS

I'm in St James's Park, and I'm pretty sure I'm looking at a swan. I'm here with my British mate Dave, and we're slightly drunk in the afternoon – a normal activity if you're unemployed and classify yourself as a writer. Swans, as far as I can tell, are white ducks with long slender necks and as violent as the Scottish. Every Brit I know has a story about a swan. And none of them are pretty.

'We were playing football one Saturday,' my friend Paul told me earlier. 'My mate Steve kicks the ball over a hedge and he runs to get it. The ball has landed in a pond or something, so we wait for him to come back with the ball. And then we hear screams. I reckon the ball had hit a bunch of baby swans, or whatever you call baby swans. We see Steve running towards us from the bushes with the fear of God in his face, and this fucking giant swan, its wings fully out like this – *Paul stands up and waves his big arms from his waist to ear level* – it was the most frightening thing I've ever seen. The swan was right on his arse, biting at him, and I swear if it had caught him he would have been pecked to death. He full on sprinted but the swan chased him relentlessly, wings outstretched until he got to the entrance to his hall of residence. He shut the door and the swan patrolled the door for ten minutes after. To this day, Steve will not go near swans. Or ponds.'

Dave points over to the swan that I am eyeing right now. 'You know they can break your arm with their necks?' I suddenly remember Kerin telling me the same thing roughly two years ago. 'It's true,' Dave rambles. 'They are bastards. You piss them off and they'll hiss and flap their wings and make weird throbbing noises.' Dave explains to me that mute swans on the Thames belong to the Queen, who actually has a swankeeper to take care of them. 'They're like simple folk covered in feathers,' he tells me.

As a Yank, I have a quick and easy solution to this frightening creature. Eat them. 'Sounds like an animal that's evolved into understanding it cannot be eaten,' I venture. 'Perhaps we should open a shop called Chicken Fried Swan. We could cut them up, dredge the meat in flour and sprinkle with a little salt. Place the swan parts in a skillet with hot fat, and then fry until golden brown. We could serve it with fruit punch, or cider.'

'No fucking way,' Dave tells me. 'Only the Queen can kill and eat them.' He then recites countless examples of people who've been attacked and/or injured by swans. One man lost an eye.

'You can't do this,' Dave tells me. He explains that swans are protected under the Wildlife and Countryside Act, and intentionally hurting or killing a swan could land you in prison. You also cannot hard boil a swan egg – nests are protected by the Act too.

'They're like dead British comedians, Greg,' Dave slurs. 'Eric Morecambe, Tommy Cooper, Bobby Davro. I'm not sure how valuable they are these days to anyone in particular, but you'd better not mess with them.'

78. NIL–NIL

(Note: this chapter contains information about the televised World Cup matches featuring England back in 2006. I thought I took decent notes, but having read over them a number of times, I realize that I was too drunk to actually keep score or follow much of the action. I apologize in advance if I get any, or all, of the facts wrong.)

I am crammed in the back corner of the King and Queen and it's swarming with fat sweaty men. My back is up against the toilet door, which makes it exceedingly hard to drink and smoke. The TV is at sharp angle above my head, so I am craning my neck. All this for a game.

It's the beginning of June, and the World Cup is under way. It's not that I follow football, it's just that I've been spending way too much time at home in my underwear. When I'm not writing boring freelance pieces for various magazines, I am, of course, surfing the internet for panda porn. I am sticking to my clothes and my furniture. I have already broken two chairs in my flat from sitting in them all day. I alternate between writing a paragraph and watching a soap opera. Elena is away visiting her folks, so my goal is to put off drinking until 5 p.m.

Thankfully, my old colleagues were nice enough to invite me to watch the match at the local pub. I jump at the chance. I need to do something other than sit at home and sniff my toes. Unemployment increases flexibility, and that's a fact.

It's actually beautiful outside, but so much for the weather. The game is on, and I quickly order a pint, and buy a pack of smokes from the machine. Sixteen cigarettes for £5.60. I think someone is playing 'Glass Tiger (Don't Forget Me When I'm Gone)' on the jukebox, but it cuts out quickly as the game begins.

This is exciting, I tell myself. Everyone here is excited.

England is playing Paraguay, I think. Paraguay is a country, or possibly a fruit juice. 'We could beat them!' says Jenni, who's as cute as a crate of puppies. She is the only one in the bar, besides me, who is drinking pink wine. She's already drunk, pointing at things not relevant to the game. The wide screen seems to be rebelling, losing the signal for brief moments, and people are groaning. I stare out of the window. The streets are empty, with the exception of a few confused tourists. At this very moment, if you were driving and ran one down one of these backpackers, you'd probably get away with it.

It's eerily quiet, so I decide to check it out. I leave the pub. The streets are deserted – even the birds are missing in action. It's as deathly still as a painting. I suppose this is what it's like after a neutron bomb: everyone is dead but the pharmacies, newsagents and betting shops are still intact. When I look down the road I imagine it must be like this everywhere; every British street, with its newsagent, pub, betting shop, pharmacy, hair salon, nail salon, Indian restaurant, and kebab house. No activity whatsoever. This is what it must be like to be inside Calum Best's head.

I hear occasional shouts from pubs all across town – every hidden pocket on every street corner erupts like a popped blister. It's a surreal experience: you look around and you see no one, but then from every direction you hear muffled throngs of shouting, as though the city is peppered with mineshafts full of trapped drunks. This must be what the Blitz sounded like to the Luftwaffe.

The weather is perfect, not a cloud in sight, and it's pleasantly warm. I see a pair of girls coming my way, one blonde and one brunette, both wearing tiny things strapped across their backs. They're technically backpacks, but they're more like backpack foetuses. I can't imagine what they fit in there.

I study their smooth, confused faces. It's clear they're unaware of the World Cup. They expect London to be teeming with commerce and conviviality, but it's like the set of *28 Days Later*. Unnerved by the silence, they peer into stores and sometimes up towards the sky. If you were a single man uninterested in football, these girls would be easy pickings. They had, after all, Canadian flags sewn on their packs. If only I had a white van.

If you're going to invade England, definitely do it during the World Cup. No one would notice, really, until the game was over. And if England had won – well, then no one would care. Unless of course the invading force was French.

Back in the bar, the TV screen is fine, but I don't watch. I'm talking to Jenni about a song by Simple Minds that I can't remember the name of. I only check the screen when I hear shouts go up around me, which I notice is a fairly common way to watch football in a pub. It seems everyone is doing it. Of the 150 or so people in the pub, only 20 are truly watching. And the rest of us are watching them.

Some tourists wander in, wearing polo shirts and black socks. They are both wearing elegant glasses, thin and particular, making them both German. They look around quizzically, and then move slowly to the bar, blocking the view of a few men, causing a rain of 'Move it, mate!' from the masses. The tourists look vaguely terrified and start ducking like panicky hens to get out of the line of sight. Their attempts to accommodate the spectators' vision only eggs on more shouting. The Germans are relegated to a clumsy version of the Chicken Dance – all the more wrong because the dance is from Switzerland.

The first half ends, and I don't know the score. During the break most of us head towards the toilet and 'have a pee'. And then more drinks. Feeling woozy, I decide to get some air. I realize I am smashed and my head is spinning. I go home and collapse on the sofa. I can't remember anything else except that England wins.

A day or so later, I go to watch the next match at the King and Queen. Dave stops by my apartment to get me.

'Football is religion here,' he says, as we walk to the pub. 'And it is probably the only time the British can act patriotic without feeling silly.'

In America, we say we are patriotic because we truly are patriotic. And, mind you, we know you mock it, but we don't care. In England, patriotism is seen as stupid, Dave tells me. Yet I look around at the men in the pub – screaming, all of them waving those little flags with red crosses, and I am perplexed.

The game starts, and we have secured a table in the rear of the pub. England is playing Sweden, apparently. The Brits have the ball, and the crowd screams loudly; some are even singing. It's weird for a Yank to see this much excitement when no one has scored. Everyone yells over a 'pass' as one player kicks the ball to another teammate.

Sweden has just scored, and the once rowdy crowd falls silent. And it stays that way for an eternity. Strange. Because there is so much scoring in American sports, when an opposing team scores the accompanying depression lasts momentarily and then dissipates. You move on. In British football, when the enemy score it's as though you've been shot through the heart. I guess that's what happens when goals are scarce: the less there is of something, the more valuable it becomes. I wonder if Brits feel this way about ice cubes.

'In England, everyone plays football, except for asthmatics who are forced to play softball,' says Dave. In the middle of his thought, he stops, and starts screaming. The Brits have scored. The momentum changes. Fans, still clutching their pints, use their other hand to make what appear to be peace signs to the screen. The pub groans like an overpacked tube carriage, as fans lurch forward, shouting and spilling their beer. It feels like something bigger than anything I could ever imagine has just happened. England has tied it all up.

I get bumped around and prop myself up against a wall. I stop watching because I can no longer see. I manage to order two more glasses of pink wine and, after a few goals, the game ends in a tie. The match is followed by polite applause, and I envision that in a few minutes I'll be back on the couch, forcing a Rustler burger down my throat.

A few days later I am back at the same pub, watching England vs. Tobago. I always thought Tobago was something you rode down a hill, but I am informed it is indeed a country. So, apparently, is 'Trinidad'. Anyway, a fan behind me keeps yelling 'fuck', his saliva peppering my neck. It feels like wasps are peeing on me.

In front of me, a huddle of balding men arch their necks upward at the screen, talking to each other without making eye contact. A drunken businessman is standing too close to me on my left, his boozy breath warming my ear. I haven't had this much male to male contact since that sleep-away camp.

A player appears briefly onscreen, and heckling commences.

'Jordan had a baby with that fucker,' Dave tells me, referring to the big-busted glamour model. 'You should see the kid.'

Dave reaches into his pocket and unfolds a sheet torn from a tabloid.

'That's Harvey,' he says. Then he folds the picture back up, and puts it into his pocket.

Bad flags hang about the pub, and I notice that the pub manager has increased the price from £4.50 to £4.75 for the pink wine I drink.

'It's always the tight bastards who get rich,' says Jenni, as she lights up one of my cigarettes.

The man with bad breath behind me starts yelling, 'Fucking hell! Come on, England!' over and over. It's actually pretty impressive that he has the energy to continue. His face is redder than a baboon's ass, and slightly less aromatic.

Zero, zero, or 'nil –nil' as you say. That's the score, I believe, at half-time. When the whistle blows, cries are heard of 'You're shit', and this variation: 'Fuck off, yer shit.'

One player, a gangly fellow named Crouch is roundly heckled by those in the pub. He looks about as far from an athlete as you can imagine. He makes Amy Winehouse look positively plump.

But then, there he goes! He heads the ball into the goal. Suddenly a horrid game has become a great one. The pub roars. England wins. People are hugging each other. I walk outside and someone has conjured up a football. A game breaks out on the street, all the players drunken men in their thirties. As they stumble about, trying to master the art of coordination, they knock over and shatter countless pint glasses. Meanwhile, other men, all woozily wasted, start texting girlfriends and drug dealers. I swear I see a few men crying. This might be the first time I have ever seen emotion like this, here, in England.

Maybe this fanatical obsession with football is born out of ambivalence for everything else. That's my flaw I guess, misplaced priorities. I worry too much about stuff like my gas bill, and not enough about football. It makes sense: if you invest all your emotional energy into a team, then it's impossible to worry about other crap. And I think that makes you, overall, a far healthier person. Contrary to what all those guidance counsellors told you, being well rounded, it seems, is bad for you. But become completely obsessed with football, and you'll probably be happy – as long as your team is winning.

79. THE FOX AND DOG

Now, I am far away, at my sister's house in a small town in California, called Benecia. It used to be the capital of the state but is now home to Exxon's massive Valero Refinery. It was also in Benecia that the infamous Zodiac killer claimed his first two victims (David Faraday and Betty Lou Jenson). I was only twelve at the time, so I swear I had nothing to do with it.

It's very early in the morning, and I'm planted in front of the television, watching England vs. Portugal. Right now, it's zero, zero, and we are seventy-four minutes into the game. The Portuguese players seem to cry a lot. 'I've never seen so many crying men,' my eighty-two-year-old mother says. 'But they're all so handsome! They are like Hollywood actors!'

It's true. These are some handsome men. And they're destroying the game, for when it's about to get moving one of these long-haired male models always falls down and grabs his knee. Faking injuries and weeping like children – it's the only way these bastards can keep from losing. My thirteen-year-old nephew Garrett walks away in disgust. No one cries in American sports.

'The Portugal players are faking it,' I tell Garrett, explaining how they're trying to kill momentum, as well as our interest. Meanwhile, the American newscasters keep returning to live segments at a British pub in Wimbledon, called the Fox and Dog.

This is the American network's way of pointing out to the rest of America that people actually care about the game, as if to say, 'Here, look at these British people, they seem to be enjoying this immensely and so should you!' An American reporter keeps interviewing a young British woman. At the start of the game her responses are coherent, but over time she starts to sway and sputter. By the end of the game, she appears to be on the verge of puking. It's a great idea for an entirely different TV show: just keep returning throughout the evening, talking to people as they get progressively drunker and drunker. Wait. That show already exists. It's called *Booze Britain*. A redundant title if ever there was one.

My mother roots for Portugal because the players are cuter. My nephew asks why there's no score, and I tell him that, 'Both teams are so equal in talent, they cancel each other out.' He realizes I'm full of shit. I then explain that 'It's not about scoring, it's how well the game is played.' He's already left by the time I've finished that sentence, going outside to the front yard to chase his sister with a bat.

Scoring is important, I know. But with football, apparently it isn't everything. And the same goes with winning. In fact, England gave up winning when it realized it was no longer a power – not with these other, louder and larger superpowers around. You'd think your country would be upset, but it's treated as a relief. Competition only creates unnecessary angst. Step out of the game, lower your expectations, and you'll have more time to get drunk. But even back in America, and doing precisely nothing, I can still feel the difference. I am back in the game, where everything happens. And I know at some point, I will be back here again. Also, I'm going broke.

The game ends in penalty kicks, and England loses. To me, the penalty kick phase in football seems the most arbitrary and pointless. It appears fair, at face value: two teams get equal opportunities to score against the other team's goalie. But it's not right, not at all. One team could play significantly better than the other, but have a really bad goalie. And so you're screwed. And during the World Cup, to lose like this must suck big time.

I imagine that roughly 5,000 miles away, there are a lot of unhappy people, sitting in pubs, staring glumly into their pints. I actually wouldn't mind being there. I bet they've got pork scratchings.

80. WASPS

Elena is back from visiting her family, and her first afternoon in London finds me sitting outside the King's Arms. She orders an orange juice. I am on my third glass of wine. I see my friend Alex approaching from across the road. I wave him over to the picnic table, and he joins me for a pint. Meanwhile Nick, sitting across from me drinking a vodka and Coke, is talking about wasps, which he talks about constantly. They seem attracted to his hair. I can't help but notice that wasps seem to play a huge role in British life, even when there are none around. 'I hate wasps, they serve no purpose,' Nick tells me. 'They aren't like bees, but they look like them.' Wasps are a common topic of conversation, I suppose in the same way French waiters are in America. They just show up, and make you uncomfortable.

Alex explains: 'When we were kids they were just always there when we went outside in the sun. The way they zip around your face is really irritating, and the sound they make is like tinnitus. Plus, they land on your food!' He waves his hand around his face, although I don't see a wasp in sight.

Like swans, wasps seem to suffer from anecdotal legends told by adults to unnerve anyone under the age of ten. 'My grandfather told me, when I was about six, that bluebottles land on your food, eat it and then puke it up again,' Alex tells me. 'I believed him and developed a minor phobia. Well, not a phobia, but you don't want them pissing around while you're trying to eat.' He pauses. 'We don't live in Ethiopia for God's sake!'

He's got a point, but Elena and I have to move on. We've got plans to do something interesting that involves horses and dressing up.

81. ROYAL ASCOT

I'm in the train station trying to find a cheap shirt. I don't know what 'Royal Ascot' is, but Elena and I are invited to attend by our delightful and attractive friend, Camilla. Camilla runs a wildly popular webzine called Popbitch that reports gossip, usually involving George Michael and anal beads. Camilla is also the kind of name you see only in England, so we feel we have to attend – if we don't, we would be betraying not just her, but the entire monarchy.

Plus, it's a beautiful Thursday in June and we figure it will be better than doing nothing on a beautiful Thursday in June. I read up on the event, and apparently the Royal Meeting is a big deal involving horses and those who ride horses, as well as people who like to get dressed up. What's conveniently left out is that although men don tuxedos and top hats, and women put on fancy dresses and ridiculous hats, they also end up passed out on lawns, often missing all or parts of their wardrobe.

At Waterloo Station, we find a clothing store where I purchase a cheap pink shirt. Nearby, at a horrible chain called Accessorize (if you've ever needed to buy a gift for a girlfriend at the airport, you know this place: it's frighteningly full of the kind of things that women generally lose the next day when they get drunk or do laundry), I buy my wife a funny hat. I choose a tiny black confection connected to a coil, which I help fasten to her head. It looks like a metallic wasp has nested in her scalp.

I had to buy a new shirt because at Ascot ties are mandatory – and my increased fatness has made it so that none of my dress shirts fit around my neck any more (it's now a 17½). I haven't worked out in five months, and I am getting pudgier and paler by the minute. I am now officially round.

Elena and I meet Camilla and a few of her drinking pals at a pub in the station. The place is full of women in hats that defy common sense and gravity. You imagine that at any moment these contraptions will self-activate and fly off with their prey gripped firmly in their claws.

Many of these women are quite large, and have wrapped themselves tightly in brightly coloured dresses, like gay sausages. Trying to get to the bar to get a drink, I find it hard to get around the shorter women walking towards me, their wide hats proving pointy and dangerous. Their dates seem to have appeared straight out of a cartoon about British men – they wear top hats, funny suits and weird moustaches, resting on their lips like overgrown centipedes. I am secretly disappointed that I don't see any monocles, something every British character in American television was never without.

We guzzle cheap white wine in a lower-ground-floor pub, and then grab some booze and sandwiches from Tesco and pile on to a train. Camilla surprises us with first class seats, which means we have our very own table. I quickly open one of our two bottles of champagne as the train departs, and it promptly blows up all over me. I look like the wrong end of a bukkake video, or the right end, depending on your predilections.

Within minutes, the train's public speaker begins a test of the emergency broadcast system, which involves a recording of a nice man counting from one to ten very slowly. This recording, we are told, would be played in case there was any malfunction with the emergency broadcast system. Except, this was only a test.

But it is the test of the malfunction system, ironies of ironies, that malfunctions. So the recording gets stuck on repeat, and runs ten consecutive times. (I believe the Beatles recorded a track based on this.) I wonder if there will be new announcement, announcing that there is a malfunction of the announcement of the malfunctioning broadcast system. Seated behind me, a lady with orange tan points out of the window. 'That's felt-em,' she says. 'It's famous for young offenders.' She's wearing a hat that looks like a crippled swan. It might still be alive. It seems to be twitching.

When we arrive, I am buzzed and already stumbling over as we cross a small bridge leading to the Ascot racecourse. Camilla explains that the racecourse has undergone an extremely expensive and time-consuming renovation. The result: the exterior resembles the IKEA store I used to frequent in Conshohocken, Pennsylvania. I suddenly feel an urge for a Poang armchair or a Docent storage combination.

The vast fields around the building's exterior are littered with drunken, well-dressed and semi-dressed people. Many of the men are sporting top hats and waistcoats, as they snooze . . . in mud. I guess this is called posh camping. 'These people aren't posh. They just get dressed up once a year, get wasted, throw up, and go home,' a woman tells me as she teeters on a plastic chair, holding a glass of overpriced champagne. I look around and see hats and a few shoes left abandoned, like orphans in the field.

I head to a kiosk to buy champagne, pulling out twenty pounds. The bottle costs over fifty, so I borrow cash from Camilla. Next to me, a woman falls over in the mud, as her heels get stuck in the wet turf. She drops a container of high-priced strawberries, but she manages to preserve her champagne from spilling.

I wander the fields, and it feels like the world's largest wedding reception – one on the verge of losing control. I climb over passed-out women, their heads still covered in those small, sideways hats. It could be a scene from *The Birds* – robins pecking away at the brains of fallen victims. The races have not even started yet.

We find a few vacant seats near another group of drunken revellers. A woman in a pink dress wanders over to them, and grabs what looks to be an empty, white plastic chair. Suddenly a man, brandishing a mobile phone, grabs her and throws her aside, as he continues talking on the phone. She is caught by a group of people, preventing her from falling into a mass of full tables. No one says anything.

Later, I see the same couple making out, in front of the toilets.

It's getting close to 5 p.m., and I realize I've been passed out for an hour. I also realize that I've missed every single race. I never even made it to the concourse, preferring to doze on the ground surrounded by empty bottles, programmes and missing shoes. I force myself into the men's toilet, and there are women lined up in there, some actually trying to pee in the urinals. Balled-up hats roll along like tumbleweeds. It's like the Wild West, but with nastier plumbing and strawberries.

Apparently, just the day before, drunken 'Topper Yobs' created a mini-riot, swinging fence posts and champagne flutes at each other. Police officers had to swoop down on the crowd, which consisted of both men and women, arresting fourteen. That must have been a fun ride to the precinct.

In America, Yanks tend to keep the low-brow and high culture in separate pots. In England, it's nice to see bad habits float upward – that even at somewhat cultured events like Ascot, you can still puke in your shoes and shit your pants. And vice versa, depending on your aim.

82. PICKLED EGGS

I am now back in London, and I meet up on the street with my friend Andy, who points us to a chip shop. We stumble in and I stare at a jar of eggs at the counter. I want one, a sign I am so drunk that I cannot wait for cooked food.

'You only get pickled eggs in chip shops, but they go with nothing else sold in the chip shop,' Andy says. 'You never say, "I'll have a saveloy, chips and an egg please, pickled preferably." Also,' he adds, 'you will never know how long they have been in that jar because a pickled egg remains freakishly brilliant white for ever. But, I love them, by the way, and buy one every time. They produce a ridiculous belch.'

83. WAVING AT PEOPLE ON, OR FROM, BOATS

As I watch my First Direct bank account slowly dwindling away, the time Elena and I spend in England seems more and more fixed. There seems to be an end in sight: if I don't start working, we've got to move. And I don't think I'll be working soon.

We walk outside and it's a beautiful day, so we head towards the river. For everyone else, it's a work day, but for us it's a holiday. We get to the Thames, hang a left and walk along the edge, and then cross along one of the bridges – the name of which escapes me because I had had seventeen pints along the way.

As we walk along the bridge, we stop and look down. A large passenger boat is drifting towards, and then underneath, us. The people in it wave. I don't know if this is an especially British thing, because, for all I know they could have been tourists, but when you're on dry land and a bunch of people go past in a boat, they wave at you. There is no exception. And you must return the gesture because, if you don't, those who did the waving will look confused. Their children will look devastated and the elderly will hate you. My British friend Chris just moved into a flat that overlooks a canal, and he explains, 'It's just about the only situation in which British people will actively seek out eye-contact and a response from strangers, and I think it's no coincidence that it takes place over a healthy distance, while in relative motion, and separated by water.' This means there's absolutely zero chance it'll lead to an approach or conversation by either party. The strange thing is that you must wave back. Maybe it's because you feel it rude if you don't, or maybe you know there might be a chance that, later in the day, you could run into them on dry land. Either way, it's a perfectly nice gesture that makes you feel warm all over, even if that feeling lasts only a second or two (like flatulence, I suppose). If you don't wave, though, the feeling that you've damaged someone could stay with you for ever. Or at least until the next boat of waving people floats by.

84. WINDBREAKS ON THE BEACH

It's the weekend, and we've been cooped up in the flat for a month, me trying to write this book, and Elena ecouraging me to write this book instead of boozing. We need a break – a quick escape from the norm for a few days, by train if possible. I call up Eoin.

'We want to go somewhere charming, maybe near the water,' I tell him, asking for suggestions. 'A bed and breakfast on a cliff. And not a lot of drunks.'

Eoin loves giving advice about where to go on trips, this despite him being a hardened Millwall fan and therefore a hearty proponent of obsessive regionalism, in that he pretty much detests anyone who lives 500 yards away in any direction.

'Broadstairs!' he announces. 'You'll love it.'

'Why?' I ask.

'Well, it's crap. But you'll see lots of wonderful deckchairs, they'll cost a pound or so to rent . . . and you'll see Brits sunbathing despite the rain. There's an arcade, and maybe even a car boot sale or a fun fair.'

I hang up and look up Broadstairs on the web. I find websites featuring pictures of cosy little cottages and cliff faces. And I must say the history behind this town in Kent actually seems pretty interesting. Located on the Isle of Thanet, it's called 'the jewel in Thanet's crown'. That has to mean something special, even though there are two other cities vying for that nickname: Margate and Ramsgate. It also had a famous resident. No, not Charles Dickens (although he lived there once) but Oliver Postgate, creator of *The Clangers*, a British kids' TV show from the seventies featuring a bunch of puppets that looked like long-nosed pigs. They whistled a lot. They're a lot like binmen.

I start phoning bed and breakfast places in Broadstairs, but due to a folk festival taking place, every joint is full. Well, except for one. After the thirteenth call, I hit the jackpot at a place with a reasonable room rate of about £35 per person. We book for Saturday and Sunday night and then run for the train.

During the quiet journey, my wife takes a nap against my shoulder. Twenty minutes later she's awake, pale, sweaty and ill. She refuses to turn back, however. This is what some people might call an ominous sign.

The train conductor announces that the train is splitting into two halves – one going to Broadstairs, the other to somewhere else far, far away. I don't hear which half of the train we should be on, and I'm not sure who to ask, since everyone seems to be asleep or pretending to be asleep. I choose to remain silent and fret for the rest of the journey. I am pulling small hairs out of my eyebrows.

We arrive, thankfully, at Broadstairs station, and grab a cab, which winds its way through some pleasant suburban streets.

'This looks nice,' I say to Elena, but loudly enough, on purpose, for the cabbie to hear it. This is a common American practice, by the way, as a secret strategy to ask for assistance in matters we don't understand.

'Don't be fooled,' comes his bitter response. 'Watch out for the youth. They congregate and cause problems.'

It's one of those things someone always says in the first fifteen minutes of any horror film.

We arrive at the hotel, a charming looking B&B across from the cold, dark sea. We rang the bell and are met at the door by a narrow old man with a high, slightly raspy voice. He greets us silently and ushers us into the cluttered hall. I smell something. Boiled Brussels sprouts?

'My wife is ill, I'm afraid, so we'll only be staying one night,' I tell the man.

He stiffens up and shakes his head.

'You'll have to go somewhere else then. I rented those rooms for two nights. If you don't want them for two, then you'll have to leave.'

His voice clicks an octave higher and he shakes. He's frightening us. I hand him my credit card, and follow him as he escorts us up the stairs to our room. When we got to the top, he stops at the door, and turns to us.

'Breakfast is 7 a.m. to 9 a.m. sharp.'

He hands us the key and then turns and leaves. We walk in, and all we can think of is . . . shit.

The room stinks of raw sewage – the kind you might imagine is full of clotted toilet paper and used condoms. We sit down on the dumpy, damp bed and wonder what to do.

'Should we complain?' I ask Elena.

'But he scares me,' she says. 'What do we do?'

Well, since we're in England, we decide to do what Brits would do. We open all the windows and run downstairs, out the front door and to the nearest bar. We head at a slanting pace, downhill toward the centre of town – a charming village filled with classic stone houses, charming shops, cosy cafes, outdoor restaurants and tacky gift centres. We walk into the first bar, and I order a whisky. It's not coming. I wait.

The servers are obese women dressed in period costumes. I am reminded of what Andy told me about the differences between American and British service:

'Miserable and ugly bar staff just doesn't happen in America. In the US, it doesn't make commercial sense to have ugly miserable people in sales. In Britain this role is not considered "sales", it's simply distribution.'

My whisky comes, and I order another while I've got the barmaid's attention. Andy is right about the aesthetics of bar service. But to me, the only thing worse than an ugly British barmaid is a pretty American waiter. I don't want to be served by someone who thinks I should be serving them.

We leave the bar, head south, and find a busy Italian restaurant looking out over the water. My wife, still not feeling well, is looking pale. I sit quietly, seeping with misery, wishing we were home. We leave and walk around town and run into a mass of kids loitering in front of an arcade, many spilling on to the street. They look no more than fourteen, and they're all smoking. Everyone in England, it seems, starts smoking before they've even learned to use a toilet.

'We start smoking at twelve,' my friend Kevin, a soldier, once told me, 'and drinking at fourteen, because we can't get decent hard drugs.'

In the US, the smoking habit is worse than making sandwiches out of puppies. And usually the most ardent smoking opponents are teenagers brainwashed by Yankee teachers. Here, though, in Broadstairs, if a kid has a mouth there's a butt dangling from it. It's nice to see teenagers doing something that really is bad for them, as opposed to doing something that's bad for the rest of us.

The teens shoot menacing stares at us – a mix of manufactured disdain and false bravado. They attempt blocking movements on the pavement, meant to unnerve anyone over the age of thirty-seven. It doesn't work. From the arcade, relentless bells, blings and buzzing noises spew forth, accompanied by the echo of bright flashing lights from odd machinery. It seems like hell designed for pattern-sensitive epileptics.

It's getting cold, so we decided to return to our B and B, which now stands for Bowel and Barf. Upstairs, the odour lingers, and we sleep above the covers, shivering in front of the open windows. We wake early, pack our stuff, and tell the proprietor we're leaving. He charges us for two nights. Hopefully, he will find the 'special gift' I've left him under the bed.

We head to the beach, and do what everyone else does on a gloomy day: rent deckchairs. I look around and see that people help combat the fledgling gusts with vertical squares of fabric – otherwise known as windbreaks. I've never seen them before. They look funny, but I wish I had one right now. They definitely serve a purpose, allowing people to enjoy an average day on a British beach without being blown into the sea.

We settle our chairs into the sand and sit down. It soon becomes cold and windy, and the sun disappears behind the clouds. I begin questioning myself. How long do we sit here? When is spending three pounds no longer a waste of money? An hour? Thirty minutes? We get up after twenty. We return the chairs and walk up the cliff steps and happen upon a funfair featuring weird games and stalls selling second-hand goods like books and hats. I start thinking of *The Wicker Man*.

I pass a sausage van, next to a mobile kennel. The proximity of both disturbs me, as does the close friendship between the proprietors. I look at the dogs available and, not happy with any of them, choose not to have a sausage.

In the middle of this circle of fun is an ambulance. I suppose, given the average age of the people around here, it's probably a safe bet it might be going home with a passenger. Elena and I buy ice-creams, and pick our way through a table full of old toys and even older tools, stuff that belonged to the once living, now deceased. Elena wants to play one of the primitive games in which you throw a hollow coconut at a bunch of bottles. Knock over the bottles, and you win the hollow coconut. Theoretically, the more people win, the more likely the game should effectively disappear.

I hand Elena 50p to play, but she fails to hit anything, so she tries again. After ten minutes we burn through a fiver. We haven't hit a thing, but I have to admit, it was fun. After we stop, a man ten years younger than me, but missing all of his upper teeth, knocks all the bottles down with one throw. He wins a coconut. He repeats the feat four times. They run out of coconuts, and the game is officially over. The man walks away, cradling his coconuts, his mouth gaping wildly.

We begin our walk towards the train station, looking forward to our flat, our own bed, and decent sanitation. Halfway there, a car pulls alongside me, weighed down with young gentlemen in hoodies. One of them rolls down the window.

'Whatchou lookin' at, mate?'

I remember the cab driver's warning. I make the mistake of saying, 'You.'

The car pulls over, and the doors swing open. These are kids, sixteen tops, white and thin as reeds. The front passenger gestures to me. I stare at them. They do nothing. They get back in the car and drive off.

That wasn't so bad.

When I get home I call Eoin, he who suggested Broadstairs as the perfect destination. We meet at the pub, and I tell him about the trip.

'Bless, that sounds about right.'

He gulps down half his Stella, and explains. 'You need trips like that to keep your expectations low. It makes for a pleasant surprise if the next time you have a great time.'

I suppose he's right. Every Brit has a similar story to mine – a nightmare weekend told with such relish that you know they would go through the ordeal again just to be able to tell the story. And although Broadstairs was a grim pageant of dreariness, it's still a fun story to tell.

More importantly, the good life requires a control group, which you can contrast with the good life. And perhaps also remind yourself how much better it is at home. That's Broadstairs.

I might go there again.

85. THE 35P COIN

I am going to see a friend of mine, an underground American comic named Neil Hamburger, opening for Tenacious D tonight. He's played at sold-out venues across England, from Birmingham to Manchester, and has been booed by tens of thousands of people along the way. He's staying with me while he opens for Jack Black's band at the Hammersmith Apollo. In return for room and board, he brings me bottles of free vodka he steals from his tiny dressing room.

I don't get Tenacious D, but I am troubled more by their fans. I see them, now, outside the Hammersmith 'Carling' Apollo, all pimply-faced teens who still masturbate into their socks.

As the lights dim, Neil makes his way on to the stage, wearing a crap tuxedo, and his hair lacquered across his head. He is wearing oversized glasses, and spilling a row of drinks that he holds in the crook of his arm. The crowd eyes him suspiciously, as he spends a handful of minutes clearing his throat. He then launches into a litany of horrible jokes, each one designed to infuriate or confuse the fans.

Within about twenty minutes the fans start throwing coins. Mostly 2p coins because that's all they can afford, having spent their cash already on vials of Roaccutane.

I've seen Neil play a bunch of times, in the US and in London, but this is the first time I've seen him play in front of thousands of people. And it's the first time I've ever seen people throw coins. It seems wrong, and it makes me wonder why decent British people would do it. I watch as men ranging from gawky sixteen-year-old boys to fat middle-aged baldies charge towards the stage and hurl a coin, and then slink back into darkness. I am standing with Neil's lovely wife, Simone, and I can tell she's ready to snap.

I ask my friend Kevin – who is British and possesses a cruel streak a few feet wide – why throw coins?

'You throw copper coins at coppers at football matches, and at anyone you don't like out of punching range. I don't know where it started but it's handy for gigs where the acts are shit. It's something we did as kids at football grounds as the mounted police attempted to bring order.'

The good thing about coins, I'm told, is that they can't be seen in the air, you don't get seen throwing them and the victim doesn't see it coming. 'They also hurt! Football matches are rife with it and the police prosecute heavily if they catch you doing it,' says Kevin as he hurls a 2p at a cat.

I suppose everyone likes the safety of being at arm's length, which explains the popularity of coins, petrol bombs, grenades and Patriot missiles. No one really wants to be up close and personal like a pugilist, punching, stabbing and charging.

When Neil leaves the stage, exiting with a final 'goodnight cocksuckers' directed at the seething crowd, I turn to Simone, who looks pretty unhappy. She is looking at a young man with a poorly maintained goatee who is gloating among his friends over nailing her husband with a coin. We walk over to him, and Simone punches him twice in the face. His temple immediately swells up, and his friends burst out laughing. 'He has the shocked, shamed look of a boy whose mum has caught him wanking,' says Dave, hiding behind me. We walk away, toward a side exit.

Moments later, the injured lad and his friends come over to express remorse and apologize. They are from Milton Keynes, says the coin thrower.

'Why is it whenever I come to London, I get punched in the face?' he asks.

'You have a punchable face,' Dave replies.

They turn out to be nice kids, who thought they could get away with something. Now they feel pretty awful. I have a feeling this kid will never forget this night for the rest of his life. He is skinny and shaking, humiliated by a woman who's taught him a lesson. I could tell he was thinking about going home to Milton Keynes.

Upstairs in his dressing room, Neil empties his pockets of about £20 in change he's picked up on stage, all hurled by the audience. Mostly 'coppers', it still adds up.

'I'm buying my wife a new sweater,' he says.

I head home from the concert. I empty my pockets, and throw

the coins on the kitchen table. I look at the three massive bowls on the counter, all filled with British coins. I have tiny cities of British coins everywhere – in the kitchen, bedroom, on every shelf. In between sipping tea and eating dry toast, I place the coins in their own separate stacks. It feels vaguely productive, but it raises the quandary: when it comes to deciding what is, and what isn't valuable, I am unsure where the cut-off is. In America, quarters and dimes and nickels are worth having. Pennies are useless. In the UK, it's trickier. For one thing, the 2p coin is almost the same size as the 50p coin. Size means everything to a Yank. And this discrepancy deeply confuses me.

I dislike 2p coins for other reasons too. They're never clean, and for some reason, they stink. I also don't like the 1p, or the tiny 5p. I have stubby, short fingers, like truncated sausages, and that makes it very hard to find and hold a 5p coin. It's a stupid coin.

I've been in London nearly two years and still coins mystify me – almost as much as tipping. I should have grown accustomed to tipping etiquette, which is 'never tip', but I still tip, and usually too much. And besides, no one gives me consistent advice about tipping. For example I have been told that you should:

- never tip black cab drivers, because they make more money than you
- always tip black cab drivers, by rounding up, as it's the polite thing to do
- never tip minicab drivers, they're crooks and rapists
- always tip minicab drivers, they're doctors or engineers from their home country, and they're supporting twelve kids.

I am in a local restaurant now, I am staring at the bill, and the tip has already been factored in. I love this, since I am terrible at maths, and easily influenced by alcohol, charming waitresses and free mints. More important, I am grateful for the handheld debit card machines, a device that has yet to hit the States. They eliminate the unnecessary step in which the server gives you the bill, you hand over your card, then they disappear with the card, and then return with the slip to sign. This eliminates one more opportunity for awkward silences between diners, and might be the biggest advance in British dining since the wooden chip-fork.

In England, maybe you don't tip as much as Yanks do because you're cheap. But cheap in a good way. Growing up in a country where you made large sacrifices during wartime and had to scrimp and save to survive, tipping probably seems like an unnecessary luxury. Like pomegranates, artichokes and fluoride.

Having said this, I think there needs to be a new coin between a 50p and a 20p. The 35p coin. That's the perfect coin for tipping, since most lunchtime meals are around £3.50, it makes perfect 'cents'!

It could have Jade Goody's face on it.

86. CHICKEN BALTI PIE

It's 2 December 2006 and it's cold and brisk – a perfect day for a football match. I'm on the tube, heading to see Arsenal play Tottenham. My mate Andy is a rabid Arsenal fan, and he has an extra ticket. I plan on meeting him in front of the tube station up the road from the stadium. When the train arrives at the stop, however, it slows down, but then continues on.

I get out at the next station, and ask an attendant for help.

'Get back on the train and go in the opposite direction,' he tells me. Then another attendant interrupts: 'No, get back on the same train you were on and go to the next stop.'

Then a cop yells, 'Just walk up the road and take a right.'

Lost and confused, I leave the station and walk up the road. I start seeing small groups of men converging, all drinking outside, on the street. Thirsty, I walk over to a cop who is busy blocking off a street.

'Sir, is it okay to drink outside?'

He laughs at me and walks away. I take that as a 'yes'.

I find the stadium, and buy a Carling from a local shop. I sit and wait for Andy, drinking and watching countless other men drinking, texting, drinking and texting – some eating chips while drinking and texting. Every person is looking for someone else. Nearly everyone is late. I decide to sit in the first 'e' of the large cement Arsenal sign. A man nearby yells into his mobile.

'No, you definitely said the L! I've been at the L for ten minutes. Where are you? The R? Oh, there you are.'

He walks over and shakes hands with another man, who had been five letters away from him.

The cops are on horses and dressed in orange, strutting like valiant sherbets. I'm told they are here to stop any violence, but they don't have much to worry about. The people here look too fat, too old and too complacent to start a scrap. And this new stadium is just too beautiful to start a rumble in. It looks like a really nice airport.

Andy arrives in a sweaty, breathless jog. The game is supposed to start in five minutes. We race to the gates.

'Tottenham haven't beaten Arsenal in thirty years!' he tells me, and I can only assume that fact is correct. 'The fans hate each other,' he adds. 'They are kept apart by fences and have to get into the stands separately.'

It's true, and we are steered like cattle along different routes to the pitch, with cops stationed along the sections as human barriers. You won't find this in the States. No one cares too deeply about anything to want to hurt someone over it, and that includes wars.

It's nice to do British stuff, I'm thinking. And today, this is me doing something British. I look at the Arsenal players' names up on the scoreboard. Fabrega, Van Persie, Eboue, Clichy. Arsenal is about as British as the Job Centre.

We have great seats, up close. There appears to be a ten-year-old girl in front of me. She turns around, and she is actually a sixty-five-year-old woman.

'They start the game early to keep people from getting drunk,' Andy says.

Still, the man next to be is fuming drunk. He is leaning on me.

'There are rules against your socks being down,' Andy tells me. I gaze downward. He adds, 'For the players, Greg.'

The game starts, and the cops sit down along the sidelines. From afar, in their orange jackets, they appear to be Jack O'Lanterns. During play we alternate between sitting and standing, unlike my experience at Millwall, where sitting was punishable by death.

A fellow named Adebayor scores with twenty-five minutes left, although he was clearly offside, I am told by the drunken man next to me, his breath warm and wet with Red Bull and vodka. I understand the offside rule, but that's not the same as liking it. I believe the rule was created for people to be aggrieved when their team is scored against. It's your consolation prize to help take the sting out of losing.

But if there was no offside rule there'd be tons more scoring. But more scoring means less time to come up with imaginative chants. And I've come to realize that chants are everything.

Arsenal fans chant Adebayor's name over and over. A man in a hooded jacket a few rows in front stands up, turns to the crowd and waves his arms like a conductor. He cups his ear and starts shouting. He is all by himself, for about twenty seconds, and then other solitary men join in. Why do men start chants? I think it's, in part, due to an inability to express affection for their fellow man. This bottled-up emotion then pours forth in the form of chanting. It also helps to be drunk.

As play resumes the same man starts pointing a finger at something on the field. No one else knows what he's on about, but he is completely certain that something has gone horribly wrong on the field.

'I love this guy,' Andy says. 'Despite the fact that out of the 60,000 people here, he is the only man who can see what really happened!' I admire that kind of certitude.

I see why Brits call football 'the beautiful game'. When it's played well, it is pretty damn attractive. I can see why people applaud for stuff that doesn't even involve scoring. Sometimes a nice pass deserves recognition, or maybe a delightful chant.

A player named Gilberto scores, and then it's half-time. I wander into the interior, and eye the food counter. I light up a cigarette.

'Sir, you must put that out,' says a gentleman in an orange vest.

On the wall menu, I notice the food is more substantial and diverse than what was offered at Loftus Road. I order a chicken balti pie and a small bottle of white wine. If I had done this at Millwall, my butt might have been passed around like a biscuit tray.

I read somewhere that over 100,000 of these pies are sold each month – I imagine a great factory, possibly underground, housing a giant machine that spits out these breaded and sealed enclosures that trap a steamy orange core of hot curry. And it is hot. I should have got a lager. I ask myself, why did I order a white wine? I think the correct answer is that I am a 'nancy boy', which is how I feel when Andy and his mates stare at me as I drink from the dainty bottle. The thought of putting curry in a pie might be the greatest union since Posh and Becks. But edible.

Back at our seats, the chanting resumes, but I can't bring myself to join in, because my allegiances are false. So my chanting will only sound weak. The drunk next to me is having an ongoing conversation . . . with himself.

'It's good they're coming . . . it's good,' he keeps saying.

He's now hugging me, and being polite, I hug back. When Arsenal scores a third goal – a penalty kick by Gilberto – the drunk shakes me like a bottle of constipated HP sauce. Cheers turn to taunts towards the miserable Tottenham fans. I try to understand what's being said (I think I hear 'Who are you' and 'You might as well go home', and 'Your support is fucking shit'. Some chants are far more sophisticated than American cheers. 'You under league in black and white?' I have no idea what that means but it sounds kinky.

It's refreshing to see grown men singing together. We don't do this in America, unless it's in a gay bar. Mostly American men just stare straight ahead when they're at a game. They don't drink as much any more, mainly because they're with their kids, or a 'client', and they're usually intent on leaving early to beat the traffic so they can get a good eight hours' sleep. I stopped attending games in America because they lasted four hours. My ass always went numb, and I'd usually fall asleep and then wake up with someone else's sock jammed in my throat.

Which is why I like soccer – sorry, football. It's now 3 p.m. in the afternoon, and I'm already home! Football is played with few time-outs, no huddles, and the clock doesn't stop when the ball rolls out of bounds. These are all great things, in that they shorten the experience so you don't get tired of it. It's based on the idea that the less you have of something, the more you like it. It's one element necessary for happiness, I think. Excess breeds boredom with the very things you initially embraced. England seems to have figured this out, and seems to ration the good stuff, so you'll never get tired of it. At least that's what I tell myself when Sainsbury's runs out of ice. And toilet paper.

87. LOU BEAL

Elena has just left for a photo-editing job in Moscow, styling a cover shoot for *Playboy*, so I have no choice but to drink. Luckily, I am already at the pub, so problem solved! I sit by the window, nursing my first pint. An old lady shuffles in with a slightly younger female friend (of about seventy), and they sit at the table next to mine. The younger woman goes to the bar to fetch a half-pint, and I am left with the old lady, who is staring at me and smiling. She leans in.

'I just bought my granddaughter a dress for Christmas!' she says, staring into my blue, frightened eyes. 'Two hundred bloody pounds! And now I have to spend the same amount for all the children.'

I nod.

'Children . . . I know what you mean.'

She cuts me off. 'That's the problem with children. They are so greedy. They never stop asking for things.' I agree, but she continues. 'I used to dance at the Palladium, for that man over there,' she tells me, pointing to an elegant man in a suit, the man with the cane who I always see at the pub. 'I used to do high kicks! But not any more. I'm ninety-three.'

She starts talking about her granddaughter again. 'She always wants to stay at mine. She never visits the other grandparents,' she adds with victory in her voice, 'but she's always at mine.'

I ask her how old her granddaughter is. 'Twenty-three.'

'Send her round to my place,' I joke but she doesn't hear me.

Dave joins me with pint in hand, and looks over at the old lady who's talking to me.

'You know who that is, right?'

I shrug.

'It's Lou Beal,' he tells me. 'She was in *EastEnders*!'

Or rather, she's the woman who played her in the 1980s. Her name is Anna Wing. Dave explains that Lou was the matriarch in town, the kind of character known for holding grudges, speaking her mind and generally annoying everyone. I don't really know her, and I am too busy thinking about her granddaughter, and what she might wear to bed.

I only watch soaps at Christmas when there is nothing else to do but watch soaps. Whenever I watch them, there is always a fist fight (or a 'punch up') or a terrible road accident that causes all the main characters to converge on dark wet pavement. The bad stuff only seems to occur around Christmas. Or maybe I think that's true because that's the only time I watch the programmes.

Soaps in America are different. The characters have better skin, teeth and hair. They have glamorous jobs, nice tits and they don't ever smoke. They have adorable children – the kind you want to torture in a basement.

On British soaps, it's pretty much a string of mundane moments punctuated by violence and car crashes. The characters have lousy jobs. But even then, this seems to work as a positive elixir for those who watch the shows.

The big problem with American television is that it seems to be designed to make you feel bad about your life. Everyone is flawless, rich, and having way more sex than physically possible. The opposite is the case with British soaps. The stuff just bubbles over with misery, and that can only make you feel better about your own life. Simply check out the men on these shows – some have pot bellies and frightening hair, and you can't help but feel your own self-esteem rise a little. At least mine does, even if it is temporary (I really have become repulsive).

I must go now. *Coronation Street* is on, and I have a crush on Rita and Stacey. Christ, I can't believe Charlie asked Tracy to move in with him. And then Deirdre snogs that guy at the pub! What a lush. And Stacy starts begging on the street for money from Fred, and then he goes and invites her home. That's just asking for trouble.

88. THE RIPPER

The *Sun* reports that the bodies of two further victims of the Suffolk Ripper were found yesterday, taking his tally to five. The dead girls are thought to be missing Ipswich prostitutes. Cops have described the shocking speed at which the fiend is claiming his victims as 'unprecedented'. He has murdered five prostitutes – all heroin addicts – in less than six weeks.

Alone in my underwear? Yes, I am. Elena has been away for a week and the need for long pants has long since faded. I am in the living room, reading the paper, drinking coffee. Thank God for serial killers – this story will carry me through this lonely month. I am obsessed with the case. I am not an expert on the criminal mind, or how to catch a serial killer, but I do have some experience with deviancy. After all, I grew up in California.

Some thoughts:

The way the British authorities handle this case is amazingly polite. When the spokesman says 'If you are the killer, please contact us, you have a serious problem. We can deal with this together' it's like they're pleading with a cat to come down from a tree.

I have noticed that every time a serial killer emerges in England, they call him 'The Ripper'. 'Jack the Ripper', 'The Yorkshire Ripper', now 'The Suffolk Ripper'. They do this even if the guy isn't technically ripping anything. I find this woefully misleading. The name should accurately describe the killer. This guy has been strangling hookers. Why not call him 'The Guy Who Strangles Prostitutes'? Straight to the point, I think.

The real problem with the overuse of the phrase 'Ripper'? It begs comparisons to the past, which only eggs on the present-day killer. In the *Sun* article, you'll find that, when compared to the Suffolk fiend, 'It took Yorkshire Ripper Peter Sutcliffe SIX YEARS to kill the first five of his thirteen victims. And his reign of terror in the 1970s and 1980s spanned a total of eleven years.' The press is turning this into an *X-Factor* for maniacs. Where is Simon Cowell for comment? He might say: 'Look, it's clear that the public loves you, but I find your performance barely passable. You just have no range.' (This comment should be followed by a chorus of boos and some heckling. Cowell will cross his arms to cover his manboobs.)

In England, the press and the public love serial killers, says Kevin (who used to kill people for the British army and relishes these stories) because, 'We always catch the killer and we are a nation of fox hunters! The hunt is now on, and we like the chase!' But there's another part to this fascination, and it's something you don't see in America: the UK is so much smaller, and you embrace your serial killers because you all think you might know him, or know someone who knows him, or maybe even know someone who knows someone who knows him or a victim. That's exciting! The UK is so small that having a killer in your midst really means something – he could be your dad or your brother!

'I've been to Ipswich, where all the murders took place,' my friend Dave proudly announces. I ask him how recently he'd been there, and he becomes very nervous and leaves.

I embrace police psychologists who voice theories in the press. The silliest shrink on the Suffolk case says: 'The killer seems to have embarked on a rampage – a kind of pre-Christmas spree.' I had no idea that serial killers actually plan their killings around the holidays. But I suppose, like buying presents, it's never good to wait until the last minute.

I know this sounds wrong, but a horrible crime spree is exactly what I need, suffering by myself during the holidays. It's what makes the UK so great. Like *Celebrity Big Brother*, a serial killing creates a sense of community built on the solid foundation of a media frenzy. It unites disparate souls in a small country who would otherwise have nothing in common. I feel, as I read the papers and watch the news, that I am part of something uniquely British – a phenomenon that captures so many different elements of modern life here in England that just don't exist in the US.

And now, there is the first arrest: a 'sad and lonely' supermarket worker who used to be a special constable. Now, if I understand it correctly, a special constable is someone who is a volunteer for the 'police auxiliary'. Where I come from, that usually means a psychopath. But this guy is innocent, it seems, and now they've arrested a cross-dressing lorry driver. I suppose that gets the special constables off the hook. But not the cross-dressing lorry drivers. Bottom line is I think I'm watching too much television. And I'm reading way too many newspapers. I am doing nothing, but immersed in everything. I'm getting to the point where I'm beginning to obsess about Martin Kemp.

89. MARTIN KEMP

I wish the Suffolk Ripper had been Martin Kemp. Because these days, that's the only person I keep seeing. I am looking at him right now. He's on TV, standing near a sofa.

In fact, every time I turn on the TV, there he is, doing sofa commercials – his flattened face stuck in a paralysis of excitement, as though reclining in a leather chair was better and more fulfilling than screwing twin fashion models. Kemp, who used to be in a horrible pop band with his brother, now hawks sofas, sofa beds and sofa-bed conversions. When you see him he is often standing (in commercials) or sitting (in newspaper ads). When he is sitting, his arms are usually raised in the air, as if to say, 'See how much fun I am having on this sofa? I prefer it greatly to my years as a rock star in Spandau Ballet!' And I, for one, believe him.

Furniture commercials are now on incessantly during the holidays, suggesting that for the previous forty-nine weeks, everyone in the UK simply stands in their front rooms, eating their meals over a tarp. Of all of Kemp's performances, here are my favourites:

- The SCS Double Discount Leather Sale
- The SCS Double Discount Sale – Boxing Day Sales
- The SCS Half-Price Sofas Christmas Delivery
- The SCS Sale, known as 'Last Few Days'

I must add that I am really looking forward to the Easter Monday Double Discount Sale. Maybe Martin will be holding a rabbit!

90. THE DRAUGHT

It's Slade again, on TV, singing 'Merry Xmas Everybody'. It's a terrific song – you can't help but feel good when you hear it. But now you cannot avoid hearing it, because it's almost Christmas.

The song is sung in every variation, from a prepubescent chorus to Tuvan Koomei throat singing. It's a wonderful song but, like everything wonderful that's been blared for 300 hours straight, it makes you want to put your head in a blender. There are plenty of British songs that have the similar effect – Wham!'s 'Last Christmas' springs to mind like a tinsel-covered aneurysm. In America, all we have is 'Santa Claus is Coming to Town'. And it sucks. British Christmas songs are there to remind you how great it is when, for the rest of the year, there are no British Christmas songs.

I was about to spend Christmas alone but my friend Andy and his wife have taken pity on me and have invited me to a place called Chester. I grab a train at Euston and head to Crewe. As the train leaves in a dense blanket of fog we are asked by the announcer to wish the train manager 'all the best', because he is retiring. I look out the window as faint outlines of trees appear like ghosts. Speaking of ghosts, we make a stop at Rugby. Rugby is famous mainly because it was where the sport was invented. Finally, the sun makes a brief appearance. Lush green fields and farms come into view as the remaining fog burns off. And then, there are sheep. I love sheep – figuratively, of course. In the train, women do the 'stumble' walk as they attempt to make their way to the toilet. They remind me of me when I'm walking home from the pub.

The train is mobbed with holiday travellers, including a fat man sitting next to me reading *The God Delusion*, by Richard Dawkins. He is holding the book up in front of his face, instead of resting it on the table in front of him. I suppose he is sending a message to fellow travellers that he, an atheist, is smarter than the rest of us who might believe in anything higher than Richard Dawkins.

I hate atheists – not because they don't believe in God, but because they believe that people who do are stupid. There seem to be more atheists per square foot in London than anywhere else, with the possible exception of hell – which may be Crewe, which is only an hour or so away.

Back when I had a job, everyone in the office claimed to be atheists. No one believed in God. They did, however, believe in ghosts. I'd never met a grown man who believed in ghosts until I came to Britain. They were not God-fearing, but ghost-fearing – often refusing to attend church, but willing to watch highly popular shows on TV about the spirit world. And there are plenty on British telly. Stuff like *Most Haunted* and *Ghost Towns* (both featuring 'psychic' Derek Acorah, with 'psychic' loosely translated as 'cock-faced buffoon') as well as spin-offs like *Most Haunted Live* lead the way in spooky crap that strikes fear in grown men who laugh at people who go to church.

'We believe in fairies and elves,' my atheist friend David explains. 'We're obsessed with Rowling and Tolkien, because those things exist, I tell you!'

I'd laugh at him if I wasn't so scared myself.

My explanation for this bizarre fascination with ghosts: draughts. Big old houses in England are so draughty that, rather than have to pay to plug them up, the Brits just blame the spooky noises and fluttering curtains on ghosts. I discover this in Chester, when I arrive at Andy's in-laws' sprawling farmhouse. As I sit in a cozy nook drinking milky tea, my ankles are freezing. I never experienced this in America – where one's entire body is warm – but here, one part always remains permanently unthawed. My first night in the guest-room bed, I realize that although the heat has been turned on only a few hours earlier, it has mysteriously been turned off again. The British somehow believe that heating is something you resort to only when absolutely necessary, like insulin or lifeboats. 'In the old days,' Kevin tells me, 'you heated only one room in the entire house. That's where you got dressed and undressed. Why heat other rooms if you weren't in them all the time?' I would have nodded in agreement but my neck was frozen.

I climb under many, many covers and finally fall asleep – only to wake up three hours later with my exposed arm completely numb. Perhaps a ghost has been sleeping on it. I desperately want to pee, but I fear exposing my genitals to the cold air would snap them right off.

But I get up anyway and, when I do, I realize every one of my footsteps down the narrow, dark halls of the house can be heard everywhere. My footsteps are causing a loud creaky sound, not beneath me, but in an entirely separate part of the house. Given the sensitivity of the floorboards and the thinness of the walls, I wonder how people manage to have sex without embarrassing themselves or offending others. This might also be why ghosts have such a strong following. How else can you explain all these grunting noises to your kids? Ghosts.

I make it through the dark hall to pee. And miss the toilet, because it's dark and I can't control the stream in the freezing air. Also, there is a picture of a relative – a handsome actor – placed exactly at eye level. He seems to stare right through me, like a ghost. Thank God for the durable grey carpeting, or I would have to mop the floor.

I return to bed and start reading a copy of the *Star*, which I purchased at the train station. I read that right now the current favourite bands in England are Girls Aloud and the Sugababes. I do believe that the monotone, grim weather is what makes Brits embrace sugary pop music. Conversely, it's why sunny Jamaica adores the slovenly and darkly depressing rhythms of reggae. It's all about balance, I suppose. Although maybe it's Nadine Coyle's tits.

I wake up early to head out for food, and it's nearly freezing in Crewe. Still, it amazes me how little clothing people are wearing on the street. The locals appear tough – one man walks like a fight in progress, his arms swinging, his legs bent. Fog envelops the road – it's gloom personified – and the vibe is industrial rock-hard nasty. Still, there are girls in skirts. I look at the shops, and all I see is kebabland, pizza places, Uncle Sam's Fried Chicken. For some reason Crewe stinks of poo – a stench that grows stronger as you head towards farm country, what my friend Andy calls, 'the home of the poor posh'.

The fact that they have land means nothing. 'Farmers got fucked by mad cow,' he tells me, which sounds like a film I once saw in Mexico. As he explains to me the problems with British milk, I see what looks like a duvet in the middle of the road. The duvet looks up at us, and moves on. It is the first time I've ever seen a sheep in the middle of the road, and it seems wholly unimpressed with us.

We stop in a pub in Tarporley, a village so grey you could lose a dolphin in it. Inside the pub, next to a fire, I watch a table of very, very old men slamming down dominoes. They are playing five pence per dot on the domino. If you don't die before the game ends, then you win.

I didn't realize Chester was built by the Romans, but I was never much for history. It always made me sleepy, just like Chester is making sleepy now. Under this heavy blanket of greyish gloom, how could you not be? I feel somnambulant, never fully conscious, as I wander the streets. I am in a town made for never completely waking up. Was Robert Mitchum from here?

We head to the Wilmington Hall Hotel, a bright and empty restaurant with red fabric stools and rugs designed to soak up liquids. It's a pattern that cannot be recreated by nature, so red wine somehow blends in. The wallpaper is a pattern of bookends, surrounding a room of small wooden tables and garish chandeliers. The decor seems to be following the theme of 'a quiet and permanent state of disrepair' or 'simply given up'. The food is great, however. I eat a terrine of chicken liver pâté, followed by a Yorkshire pudding the size of my head.

'It's a big portion,' warned the elderly waitress, 'but you're probably used to that, aren't you?' I stare at the pictures of horses on the walls. We are the only diners in the main hall that evening.

We return home and I sit on the sofa. I accidentally tear the lace off one of the pillows. I try to hide it so my hosts won't find it. I would blame it on one of the two dogs but, being British, the hosts would probably throw me out for that. They adore their dogs – even the one that keeps biting my crotch.

91. THE FOX HUNT

In the morning, Caroline's mum makes me a bacon 'sarnie', which is short for sandwich, although I don't get the logic. Caroline's mum is, according to Caroline, the 'poshest person I know'. She is a nice woman, who employs the phrase 'jolly good' with the same frequency that some of us breathe. She makes an excellent sandwich – er, sorry, 'sarnie'. I will never get this right. I'm told you can't have a chicken Caesar sarnie, but you can have a bacon sarnie. That's because sarnie is southern for sandwich, but only if it contains bacon. Buttie is northern for sarnie. A chip buttie, the strangest idea ever for a sandwich, is often improved with salt and vinegar. A bap? That's a white soft bread roll. I realize that if you have a bacon sandwich on white bread, it screams for red sauce. But if you toast the bread, then it must be brown sauce. It all makes perfect sense.

We are now going to the Cheshire Foxhunt. Fox hunts are illegal, so we have had to do some research to find out where it actually is. Our research entails Andy's wife calling her sister, and asking, 'Where is the fox hunt?' She gives us the location, and then tells us that the Cheshire Foxhunt is one of the oldest, if not *the* oldest, hunt around, dating back to the 1700s.

We drive to the spot at the top of a muddy, narrow road, and get out of the car. The riders on horseback eye me suspiciously. I don't look like one of them. Not by a mile. Andy suggests they probably think I'm an 'anti', someone opposed to fox-hunting who comes here to stir up trouble and make rich people feel bad. I deflate their suspicions by greeting each rider with a hearty hello and waving the carcass of a dead fox. They tip their helmets or shoot me a wide grin. We watch the dogs swarm and the riders follow. The chase begins alarmingly fast, as the twenty-five or so hounds take off and I scamper to move out of the way of a few very polite horsemen.

We hop in the car and follow a posh guy in a red jacket on a horse. We figure he must know where he's going, so we stick with him. But we get lost. I can see the horseman riding over some farmland, but there seems to be no real order as they are probably going to end up back on the road. Still, it looks like fun. Seriously, if you weigh the absolute pleasure derived by all the horses and dogs, versus the terror of one fox, I think it's more than a fair trade. And what are foxes anyway? They're nothing but lazy dogs. If they could have tried a little harder at being domesticated – or shown a little more affection to women and children – they'd be the ones doing the hunting. Basically, they're just dogs with ASBOs.

92. THATCHED ROOFS

We park off the side of the road and climb up on to the bonnet and watch the dogs sniffing around. A young girl on a horse returns, crying. I think it's time for a drink. We get back in the car and head to Caroline's sister's for coffee – an exciting moment for me because she lives in a house with a thatched roof. I have never seen a thatched roof, ever. I am told a thatched roof can last seventy years, but I assume that when they break down elves, fairies and woodland creatures will come to fix them. I read that there used to be a million thatched buildings back in the 1800s, but now there are only 24,000. I wonder where all of those folk moved to. My only guess would be canal boats.

'Only rapists and tinkerers live on canal boats,' Andy explains to me while driving along a canal, and I nod agreement. They seem to me, anyway, like floating bedsits – the initial dream the owner had of travelling in them discarded long ago in favour of sitting quietly and weeping. I imagine now that each boat is filled with cheap sausages and pornography.

'My nan ran off with a bloke and moved to a canal boat in Nantwich,' Andy adds.

Perhaps that's where his bias against canal boats originates from.

'Rapists and street performers,' he mutters to himself. 'Rapists and parfooglers, the lot of 'em and don't let anyone tell you different.'

I don't know what a parfoogler is, but it can't be good.

We drive along country roads among stately brick villages; it's rainy and grim as we make our way through towns called Audlem and Whitchurch. I see a sign that reads 'secret bunker', defeating the purpose somewhat.

We stop at Tracey's thatched house in proper horse country. Tracey introduces me to her donkey called Josh – a name normally reserved for mediocre Hollywood actors. The donkey had been sleeping near his own filth and piss – also a practice normally reserved for mediocre Hollywood actors. Inside the tiny house, I feel sleepy, as mince pies are passed around. I don't get mince pies, because I assume they are meat, but they aren't, and I don't know what's in them. Pudding, perhaps? So I eat chocolate coins instead. While we sit, Tracey's husband, Rob, spills the beans and tells her what he got her for Christmas.

A goat.

We head to another pub, across from St Boniface's Church, with a ghostly cemetery, featuring towering gravestones. I read in the paper that Bono is given an honorary knighthood, at which point an old Brit in the bar remarks, 'They're giving knighthoods away like bloody toffees!'

Slightly drunk, I head to the railway station to go back to London. An earlier cancellation of a coach has filled the train, and there are no seats. As I go to the luggage rack and place my case on it, I see what appears to be a ghost. My bag moves back towards me, and there's a ten-year-old boy sleeping under the case rack. He tells me to fuck off. And I do.

93. HIGH TEA

I get the phone call. After a few interviews in the States, I've been offered a new job in television, hosting my own show. There's just one hitch: the show is in New York City. I know what this means. I won't be enjoying my serene decline much longer. I have to get back in the game.

I want to cry, mainly because *Celebrity Big Brother* is starting, and if my new employer has his way, I will probably miss the finale. It's only the second day, and Ken Russell has already accidentally exposed himself. I can't imagine what he'll do in a week's time, but I imagine it will involve faecal matter and a pipe.

I somehow can't bring myself to the thought of leaving England. The idea of leaving this, for that, is scary. I may be going broke and expanding to the size of a small town, but on the whole that's not so bad. If New York is the 'city that never sleeps', then London is the 'city that prefers to lie around all day'. And that's me all over.

I would rather embrace the warm fuzzy pillow that is a former empire, than the cold remote reality of Manhattan – a machine that refuses to fall behind. My wife's flight is delayed a few days due to bad weather, I'm alone, and it's closing in on New Year's Eve. I am inconceivably sober. So what should I do? There is only one thing, really, to do. Have tea.

I pack a small bag and head out to Marylebone Road, and walk until I find a bus stop off Baker Street. I want high tea, so why not go to the oldest tea house in the UK? I hop on the next bus to Oxford, home to colleges, college students, and pipe-smoking cardigan-wearing vessels known as professors. The bus is very clean and, with the exception of six Japanese tourists, it is very empty. This, after all, was the day before New Year's Eve, and most people were probably either in a carbohydrate-induced coma, or saving up their liver enzymes for tomorrow.

The bus, warm and cosy, has a bathroom, or rather a 'toilet', at the back. I've never used a toilet on a bus in my life. But the day is still young. There are few cars on the road and, within an hour,

I arrive at Oxford and find Kevin, the former SAS soldier, on the high street. I can't miss him, because he's wearing his thick red jacket. He wears the puffy thing everywhere. We walk down a very narrow and old road, possibly the tiniest road ever made, made even tinier by the two solid yellow lines painted within it, eliminating all but Kate Moss from walking down it.

Still, there is a cashpoint. Sadly, wherever you find a wall, you will find a cashpoint embedded within. It's a weird thing to see this most rustic of walls penetrated by an ugly mechanical box full of money. Cashpoints, it seems, make no effort to blend in. They are like German tourists.

I withdraw £40 and we head to a pub. It's called the Bear Inn, and it's full of old men and a large table of gesturing Japanese tourists. I ask Kevin what the hotels are like around here, hinting perhaps that he might offer me a place to crash. An ex-soldier, he dismisses the idea of ever having to look for a hotel.

'Last week I slept in a hedge. It's the best place to sleep, especially if it's within a roundabout. Then it's the safest place ever.'

He tells me that when he drinks too much and it's too late for him to get a train home, he finds a hedge in a roundabout.

'That's the thing about England you don't understand, Greg. Trains weren't made to run all night. Back 150 years ago, that was unnecessary.'

So when he's caught without a bed or a roof, he finds a hedge. He calls them 'urban sleepovers'. He chooses dense bushes away from the road.

'I like to go deep in parks where only the fucking hard rapists go! They'll never find you in there, and this only works if you're not at all phased by hard rapists generally. Roundabouts are ideal as they are free from humans. Bushy roundabouts that are slightly built up and hilly are my ideal choice. You can sleep all day undetected in those.'

Kevin always wears his red down jacket, he tells me, because it's waterproof, warm and has a hood.

'I lay a small amount of dry material down as ground insulation, if I'm sober enough, or steal a tramp's cardboard box. I always steer clear of alleyways, bins and anywhere else that hookers, pimps and vagabonds may be lurking.'

But more important, he adds, the police will never randomly

venture into roundabouts or bushes. 'It's cheap and convenient, best applied in fairer weather.'

I sit quietly, and ponder my short-term future.

'But Greg,' Kevin finally says, 'you're always welcome to stay at my place. We have a spare room.'

We head over to the Mitre, another pub, and 'the most famous residential hotel in Oxford'. There are numerous pictures of Churchill on the wall – beneath them, old people are slowly getting drunk. The toilet door makes a squeaky noise, like a geriatric fart. Outside the trees appear handicapped, propped up with what look like crutches, with the same kind of lightweight elbow crutches people use. Given the state of health care in England, I wonder how long it took for that tree to see a doctor.

We go to a place called the Grand Cafe, finally, for high tea. Kevin tells me it's the oldest tea house in the country, renowned for its tea, tea snacks, and intimate atmosphere. But when I get there, it's not what I had imagined it to be. With mirrored walls, it looks more like a dance club for seniors. The menu features white-peach bellinis – a drink made from peach chunks, sugar and lemon juice. Somehow, this doesn't feel like high tea. It's more like Secretary's Night at TGI Friday's. The jukebox comes on, playing the song 'Cum On Feel the Noize'. I'm waiting for the karaoke to begin.

The scones arrive, and I smother them with butter, jam and clotted cream. What a combination. Nothing but fat, carbohydrate and sugar. How can Americans be called pigs when you serve this up? I think I can hear my arteries pleading for mercy, or at least, a quick death.

Slightly drunk, I guzzle my tea like beer. We leave and decide to sneak into Exeter College. I walk along its beautiful, perfectly maintained lawn. 'If you step on it, you're fined £50,' says Kevin. He proceeds to do a jig on it. We enter the thousand-year-old chapel, which still looks beautiful, despite the construction inside. A man urinates against the chapel. The acoustics are amazing!

We stumble into yet another pub called the King's Arms. Students proliferate like bugs, in blazers, ties and with baleful expressions. In the restroom, there is graffiti in Latin. Above it, someone smarter (but also stupider) has written, 'this is incorrect'.

There is a longer essay on the door, written by a woman about her ex-boyfriend. It's almost a thousand words or so. The answer below: 'I bet you're an American! Stop pouring your heart out and fuck off.'

We sit at an old table, and I point out to Kevin that it is crooked.

'This table is probably older than your country,' he replies.

We continue to drink until closing, mocking students and pounding vodka. I don't remember much else. We jostle some students. And later I pass out on a mattress on the floor of Kevin's house. He sleeps in a hedge in his garden.

I grab a bus back in the morning, feeling very sick. I can feel the onslaught of diarrhoea, the urge that somehow always seems to outpace your body's attempt to find a WC. I run to the toilet in the back of the bus and squat down just in time. The bus goes over a rough road and I am thrown off the seat. And then, the light goes out and I am stuck there, in darkness, covered in my own filth. Still in darkness I feel around for toilet paper – and I find something thick and damp. It's all I've got.

As the bus winds its way back to London, I can't help but feel sad. Everything is grey and cold, and I spot one sheep alone in a vast green field. It is now New Year's Eve. I eye the falafel shops, the pizza joints, the cash and carrys along the Westway, and I feel grimly alone. It quickly dawns on me that I have lost my umbrella. I suddenly remember what I used in the bus toilet.

94. NEW YEAR'S DAY PARADE

It's now the 1st of January, and I'm standing on the steps at Piccadilly Circus, getting ready for the New Year's Day parade. I'm surrounded by Americans, Asians and Germans but very few, if any, Brits are in sight. The American man, from New Jersey, is insistent on getting the best view, and keeps knocking me backwards. The German couple next to me speak in German, sounding like they're plotting something. Cops come in on horses and orange vests, and the Japanese take pictures as fire trucks rumble down the streets. It's a cold morning, and I finally see a few Brits – they're the only girls wearing short skirts without tights. I remember my friend Jenni once telling me that girls who don't wear tights have chlamydia, and I chuckle. A man blocks my view with a pizza sign. People seem slightly pensive, craning their necks. Small carts motor by. People excitedly take pictures, before realizing the small noisy cars are advertising vacation packages to Greece.

'That's not very exciting,' says one woman, already looking at the pictures she's taken on her digital camera.

Motorbikes follow, some with sidecars, drizzled in tinsel and flags. I hear a marching band, green pom-poms bouncing above them. I see the tops of tubas, as they start playing a song that sounds oddly familiar. I get up on my toes and see that it's an American marching band from an American high school. The song they choose to play: 'We're an American Band', by Grand Funk Railroad.

Following the band, right on their asses, in fact, is a group of old men in berets, some Bobbies and men in horse-drawn carriages. But they can't go any further, because the American band has paused to do a drum solo. A double-decker bus pulls in behind them, filled with a few people dressed as pirates. I hear bagpipes. People start cheering. For bagpipes.

They perform a medley of hits, including 'Oh! Susanna' and 'They'll be Coming Round the Mountain'. Next up are fat girls in tiaras, in a small open-topped cart designed for fat girls in tiaras.

A large man arrives on a Penny Farthing – one of those really old bicycles that you only see in paintings and on postage stamps. The crowd looks up as he passes by . . . and then suddenly their heads drop down, and they let out a groan. It appears the man has fallen off.

Happy New Year.

95. THE NEW PICCADILLY CAFE

A white-haired man walks by my table and I wave him over, menu in hand.

'Can I order please?'

'No,' he says. 'I'm executive. You need labour.'

I'm sitting at a freshly wiped and still damp table at the New Piccadilly Cafe. The menu is as old and as flimsy as a historical document normally kept under glass in a museum – an orange thing ready to dissolve in my hands. Many of the meals have been crossed out or stickered over with handwritten specials. I peer over towards the men in the formal waiter uniforms hovering in the corner. They're talking, and their shoulders are adorned with red epaulettes. The white-haired man points over to them.

'When they're finished with conversation, they will see you.'

I am enthralled by the strange complexity of the dishes listed – meaning, I have no idea what they are. Cassata Siciliana, with semolina and rice pudding added ... escalope Piccadilly garni ... steak pizzaoili garni. The fancy names don't seem to jibe with the yellow Formica tables, the tattered theatre posters on the walls and the postcards plastered in every corner. The waiter comes over and, being a true American patriot, I ask him about the 'steak American garni' for £8.50.

'I tell you,' he says. Then he walks away.

He returns a few minutes later and says, 'Steak with green beans and a fried egg on top.'

I order a Coke, which comes in a plastic glass with no ice. It is followed shortly by a plate of egg, sausage and chips. The waiter drops off the brown and red sauce, along with a folded napkin. Across from me, a middle-aged man shares a bottle of wine with himself, talking to the manager about the siege of Vienna. I drop a knife on the floor, and the waiter scrambles over to replace it. I sit quietly and stare at the comfortable clutter in this dark shady box on Denman Street. This place is a frozen-in-time feast for the eyes – a strange horseshoe-shaped menu folding around a basic wall clock, the red vinyl booths and uncomfortable flat benches, overgrown plants, a huge ugly lamp and an out-of-place coat rack, bow-tie shaped red plastic lights, and behind the counter among the clutter you see an old mixer and a grey cash register. The mismatched furniture and detritus gives me the impression you're dining in the middle of an auction of someone's valuables, freshly deceased. The only thing that reminds you it's 2006 are the tacky posters for *Mamma Mia*, *Spamalot* and other musicals, which infest every nook.

This was the first and only real old-school cafe I found when I moved to London way back when, and I could never seem to find it again. Kerin took me here one afternoon, explaining to me that this was one of Europe's most famous cafes. The sign outside seems like it has been resurrected from a junk bin, stained and appearing to rust – it promises 'quality food served all day'.

'Nothing has changed about this place,' Kerin once told me over an omelette in one of these red booths, 'since it opened a zillion years ago.'

He told me that three years ago, and now I can honestly tell you, the place hasn't changed in a zillion and three years.

Kerin said the cafe was going to close, for good, mainly due to massive rent increases, which seem to knock out dozens of old cafes, making room for Starbucks, which, when you think about it, is the antithesis of the New Piccadilly. Sleek, no sharp edges and built to be replicated identically in any part of the universe, Starbucks is designed to be simultaneously identifiable and identity-less. You can't make two New Piccadillys though, and sitting in one of its shaky benches now, I find it pretty impressive they were able to make one. The place, like England I suppose, seems to be in a murky, but no less jubilant state of disrepair.

But the New Piccadilly Cafe is still here, and I hope it will be here far longer than I will. But I don't know. I've already read in the paper that, in just a matter of months, you'll no longer be allowed to smoke in pubs any more. A little part of Britain will die when that happens. It may save your lungs, but I wonder if it's a fair trade-off. Lungs are overrated. I now wonder if the New Piccadilly will be next.

I've just returned from my third and final rehearsal for a TV show filmed in New York. It looks like I'm moving back, and moving fast.

I dig into the sausage – warm on the outside, and a fiery mushy hell on the inside – and I burn my tongue once again. The French fries are wilted, soggy and serve only to poke the eggs for a yolky sauce. I am the only person in this place now, on a Wednesday afternoon, and I sense death.

From the sidelines in London, I must now return to the game, and it is a relentless one, where life is tabulated by victories that are almost always quickly forgotten. Meanwhile, the defeats follow you for ever, only temporarily abated by vodka and/or drugs. That is New York. Here in London, it's the reverse. The grandeur and beauty of past triumph is indeed past. But for some reason, you are allowed to bask in the glow of that fading star. It is a feeling so warm and comforting, like the decaying embrace of the New Piccadilly . . . that failure seems only a footnote – fleeting and unimportant, and easily erased by a pint on the corner of Riding House Street. Or anywhere, for that matter. The New Piccadilly might be a dying thing, but somehow life never feels any better, or slower, when you're sitting in a cramped booth sucking on the world's worst milkshake.

EPILOGUE

New York, New York. Fourth of July, 2007. I've been back in Manhattan for five months, working on a television show. From my office space in Manhattan, I am watching the news of the attempted car bombings in London, and wishing I was there. I suppose I have 'terror jealousy', a new phenomenon coined by my British mate Dave, who's in a London pub, smashed.

'America wishes it had all the stuff we've got going on right now. Because when it's here it's small and real and nuts,' he says. 'When it's where you are, it's big and scary and like something from a film. We're Begbie from *Trainspotting*. You're the rapper from the Black-Eyed Peas.'

That's England and the US, in a strange little nutshell.

Dave's friend 'Energy' Ben, works in the office next to Tiger, Tiger, one of the targets of choice for the bombers. They've all got the day off to go drinking, and, even better, their bosses have given them a 'drinking allowance'. In America, you'd be offered counselling. In England, it's pints.

So they all go out and get smashed in Soho. It's a great day for the war on terror, but mostly for getting really drunk.

I ask Dave why his friend is called Energy Ben.

'Mostly because he eats lots of party Smarties. Anyway, Happy Fourth of July. I can't believe you guys come together to celebrate the film career of Will Smith, but it's kinda nice.'

I know why I'm sad, and it's not terror jealousy. You know you love a place that, when it's in the midst of chaos and threatened with annihilation, you really wish you were there. And I do. I just miss that damn place, and wish that one day I'll be able to return. If it'll have me, of course.

AFTERWORD WITH JOHNNY ROTTEN

I'm back in Benecia, California – it's late August, and Elena and I are visiting my family. It's a really sad thing when a fourteen-year-old boy is a head taller than you, but for me, it's not just sad, it's a reality. My nephew Garrett, who I haven't seen in six months, has experienced a growth spurt that has relegated me to a pudgy Smurf in his presence. He also has a girlfriend, and listens to 'emo'. I can deal with the former, but not the latter. It's for that reason that when Garrett's birthday approaches, I purchase *Never Mind the Bollocks, Here's the Sex Pistols* as his gift.

I don't think he wants it, but I don't care. When I got the Sex Pistols' debut twenty-odd years ago, I was only fifteen or so, and it scared the hell out of me. For three months I kept that ugly pink record away from my other records, as though it had an infectious disease that could ruin my ELO LPs. If you were looking for something that sounded positively evil, you couldn't find anything better than Johnny Rotten's voice.

The first time I heard it, I was sitting on my twin bed, listening to *Holidays in the Sun*. The guitars, the drums and that voice seemed so alien, so aggressive, that I got up and lifted the needle off the record. I had played that song for only forty-five seconds, and it was over. I couldn't listen to that album again – and never, ever by myself.

Of course, that record continued to sit in the corner of my room, taunting me, and when I returned to play it, I got it. And for six months I played the damn thing to death. This amazing rock record, in a matter of months, changed the way I looked at the world and turned me into an apostle for the Pistols, and punk rock in general. I cut my hair, wore the closest approximation to a punk wardrobe I could find in our local mall (I purchased parachute pants, and a sleeveless shirt made from latex, and loads of badges), and ended up resembling a shorter version of Nicolas

Cage from *Valley Girl*. The Pistols were playing Winterland, in February 1978, and I was fourteen. I had no driver's licence and no adult would take me. To think the king of rock and roll was only twenty miles from me – and I didn't take a bus.

So now it's late August 2007, and I'm back in Manhattan doing my TV show. I've just had my make-up done for my pale, puffy face and I'm signing my wife in at the front desk at Fox News Channel. As we leave with my wife's pass, we turn a corner and I see him exiting through the security turnstile. He's wearing a bright-red vest, his hair is corn-on-the-cob yellow, and he's smiling. I go up to him, and introduce myself.

'Johnny, I'm Greg Gutfeld, the host of the show you're on.'

Johnny shakes my hand and says, 'Let's get a smoke!'

He offers me a Marlboro red. He lights my cigarette and my hands are trembling. Thoughts go through my head – all suggestions of things to say that might make him like me, or at the very least, make me feel less nervous. But I don't have to, because before I say anything, he says, 'I really like your show! It's refreshing! Breath of fresh air! Nothing wrong with that!'

So we smoke another cigarette, and I tell him that I really miss living in England, and does he ever miss it, now that he lives in southern California?

'Sometimes,' he says, 'but there's no community there any more. All you see is St Arbucks. I need community, a neighbourhood.'

I tell him I prefer living in England to New York.

'That's because things are open, more relaxed in London,' he tells me. And adds, 'You have me to thank for that, mate.'

I spent most of the afternoon prior to the show wondering what to call him. Was it his real name, Lydon, or his adopted name, Rotten? Turns out he's more comfortable with Rotten, especially since he's reuniting with the rest of the Pistols in a few months for a show on the 30th anniversary of the release of the *Bollocks* album.

We go back into the studio and do the show. Rotten is absolutely hilarious – the perfect guest. Afterwards, I ask him to go drinking, and he and his friend Rambo meet us at a local Irish bar. I order them both double sea-breezes, which they down easily. After drinking in the back room for several hours, I ask him about whether or not Sid Vicious was capable of killing Nancy Spungen.

'Everyone was capable of killing her. It was like *Murder on the Orient Express*. So many people hated that girl, there were just too many suspects.'

Over the night we manage to agree that Steve Miller's *Fly Like An Eagle* was an amazing album, but we disagree over the Smiths, of whom he says all the guitar work is entirely off-key. This, from Rotten. In the middle of a cigarette he explains to me the secret behind the success of Public Image Ltd's inventive guitar work.

'I heard it on an old Wishbone Ash record. Not a very good one, but the guitar sound was amazing.'

He then ragged on about Sting for his constant obsession with Tantric love, the sexual practice in which you hold off orgasms for hours.

'Have you met Trudi Styler?' Rotten asks.

Later, when we are talking about football hooliganism, he gives me an in-depth look at his teeth, which he spent twenty grand on, then lost one tooth, leaving a gap front and centre. On close examination it looks like the entrance to the Pirates of the Caribbean ride at Disneyland. After all the fighting in his life, he finds it funny that he lost this tooth to a cherry pit.

He loved my wife, Elena, and was shocked that we were married, saying, 'I thought you were a saucy bugger.'

He told me how weird it is go to parent/teacher conferences in California. He hates the Left there, and wishes everyone spoke better English.

Throughout the night British folks come to our table to get him to sign napkins, get photographed with him, or get a peck on the cheek. At one point, some of the drunker men try to drag him to another bar, asking him why he bothers drinking with Americans when he should be with Brits.

'Fuck your nationalism! We're all going to end up in the same place!' he tells them, as his burlier friend Rambo pushes them along. He then pats me on the back, and says, 'Let's drink! This is fun!'

ABOUT THE AUTHOR

Greg Gutfeld was born in 1964 and grew up in Sat Mateo, California. He has worked in magazines for a good chunk of his adult life, including *American Spectator* and *Men's Health*. He is ex-editor of *Maxim* in the UK and now works for Fox News, making a name with his news show *Red Eye with Greg Gutfeld*. Check out Greg's blog:

www.dailygut.com